The Air I Breathe
It's Classified

By

Bearnairdine Beaumont

The Air I Breathe

It's Classified

by

Bearnairdine Beaumont

ISBN: 978-0-9933025-0-3

Published by Bearnairdine Beaumont in conjunction with Writersworld. This book is produced entirely in the UK, is available to order from most book shops in the United Kingdom, and is globally available via UK-based Internet book retailers and www.amazon.com.

Copy edited by Ian Large

Cover design by Bespoke Book Covers

www.writersworld.co.uk

WRITERSWORLD
2 Bear Close Flats
Bear Close
Woodstock
Oxfordshire
OX20 1JX
England

☎ 01993 812500
☎ +44 1993 812500

The text pages of this book are produced via an independent certification process that ensures the trees from which the paper is produced come from well-managed sources that exclude the risk of using illegally logged timber while leaving options to use post-consumer recycled paper as well.

If you want to contact the author directly, please go to www.aerotoxicteam.com or email aerotoxicangel@gmail.com

Disclaimer

The entire content of this book is based upon the life, experience and opinions of the author unless otherwise stated. Short excerpts of studies, articles or other quotes are based upon the opinions of the respective author who retains full copyright as marked, and/or they have been quoted under the Fair Use *law and are intended for educational purposes only. However, the author has endeavoured to list all respective publishers and authors at the end of the book. The information in this book is not intended to replace a one-on-one relationship with a qualified, registered and licenced health care professional/physician and is not intended as medical advice or diagnosis. It is intended as a sharing of knowledge and information drawn from the research and personal experience of* Bearnairdine Beaumont. *The readers are encouraged to make their own health care decisions based upon their research and in partnership with a qualified and licenced health care professional. The author does not intend to give the one and only correct answer or advice of how to regain health after exposure to contaminated cabin air. Some names have been changed or are not mentioned.*

If you comment please be kind.

Dedication

For my Parents with Love:

Captain Walter Alexander Baumann, R.I.P.

Caroline Elisabeth Renée Baumann-Watts, Air Hostess, R.I.P.

Contents

Author's Contemplation

Looking back as if through a veil sometimes, a witness to my own life, I remember one fascinating, sometimes challenging, chapter after another. I have learned that events and things can happen which we ourselves cannot possibly imagine and which we certainly cannot influence.

Circumstances can have a force, sweeping us up by events, which we do not understand and are powerless to stop. Things can happen and you feel them happening, but you have no connection to them and certainly no key to the cause or the meaning of them.

Yet I continue to live and to enjoy life, both looking back and moving forward.

Foreword

Journalism is printing what someone else does not want printed.
Everything else is public relations.

(George Orwell)

While investigating and researching the issue of contaminated cabin air since 2008 I have personally met more than some hundred individuals who all have one thing in common: they became victim to toxins present in the cabin air aboard modern aircraft and they became seriously injured. This, in most cases, changed their lives forever. One of them was Bearnairdine Beaumont, a former chief flight attendant and the author of this book. While industry representatives, and among those even professionals, who claim to have a profound medical background, are still denying that these symptoms may be associated with anything these people inhaled aboard any aircraft, there is overwhelming evidence to the contrary.

When I personally met Ms Beaumont for the first time it was at an airport, of course. I did not assume that this meeting and our flight together from Frankfurt-Main to Dublin would also change my life, my previous 100 percent loyalty and my deeply-founded respect for my long time employer, a renowned German public broadcast station. I was in the process of working on a TV documentary about contaminated cabin air, and Ms Beaumont was one of our carefully selected protagonists. We had previously talked for hours via Skype and on the phone and she even submitted to me her personal medical records and findings to substantiate what she claimed had happened to her.

As our aircraft was parked out on the ramp we were taken on a short bus ride to reach its position. When we approached the aircraft on the tarmac I noticed that there was a significant change in Ms Beaumont. She became quiet and tense, her mouth and nose were covered by a carbon filter mask, a 'precaution' as she told me. In her handbag she even carried a heavy-duty respirator mask, one of those required by firefighters and workers in chemical plants. Other passengers apparently did not take any notice of this unusual appearance, nor did anyone make any attempt to inquire. For a moment I visualised mentally how it would be if such equipment would be included into the on-board safety briefing routinely held by the cabin staff, such as the demonstration of the life vests. I need to mention here that it is a widespread misinterpretation that in case of what the industry calls a 'fume event' the on-board passengers' oxygen masks would be deployed or be of any help. They will only be deployed in case of loss of cabin pressure and the amount of oxygen provided is very limited, and on top of that you will still breathe in what is in the cabin air. But this worst-case scenario, in which thick smoke limits the visibility and makes breathing difficult, is – according to renowned scientific opinion – very likely not as severe as the effects of continuous low level exposure to the compounds you breathe aboard an aircraft.

Today in our daily life we are surrounded by many substances and compounds, some of chemical origin and even toxic or carcinogenic and an increasing number of people are reacting in an extremely sensitive way to such substances. Also we learned that genetic variations in humans make some people more susceptible to such compounds and they may show severe symptoms, while others seem not to be affected at all.

We also know that inhalation is the most effective way of administering something into the human body and into our bloodstream, second to an intravenous injection. Depending on what these substances are, some will even have no problem travelling through your body within a few seconds, penetrate the blood-brain barrier and show effects on your brain cells and your nervous system. This is specifically the case with organophosphates, a family of chemical compounds originally designed as warfare materials – such as for example the well-known nerve agent sarin.

It was much later in time that these organophosphates became widely used as flame-retardants, pesticides and last, but not least, as an additive to the engine oil of jet aircraft engines. But, when these fluids were approved for general use in aviation nobody even dared to think that one day millions of people aboard aircraft would inhale the heated or 'pyrolysed' fumes of such compounds, as the air will be taken straight from the jet engines and, without any filters other than the lungs, into those individuals who inhale these chemical cocktails. Also, until today, there is not even a requirement for a simple sensor within the high-tech environment of the most advanced flight decks of modern aircraft, which would warn the pilots that something is getting into the breathing air that could be harmful. Some industry experts claim that their measurements do not exceed any workspace limits for specific compounds. What they do not mention here is that these standards do not apply to the confined space of a pressurised metal tube, travelling at 38,000 feet and almost at the speed of sound with no chance to get outside or even open a window, as it would be the case in every office or industrial factory building on the ground.

Unfortunately, and to my surprise, the responsible decision-makers within my former network decided to exclude Ms Beaumont's case completely from being broadcast on television. They even went so far as to take away my authorship and changed the film to their own liking, and finally aired it without getting my approval or seeking my expertise for any of these changes. But what I found most disturbing and would have never dared to imagine was the fact that it wasn't any of my former colleagues who advised me about this sudden, but significant change. It was an email from the communications department of a major German airline, the very same airline that also happened to have been the former employer of our protagonist Ms Beaumont...

Working as an investigative journalist does not necessarily make you many friends, especially not in the areas that are the subject of your research and reporting. Since I started to shed some light onto this dark story, which I believe is one of the aviation industry's biggest 'dirty secrets' and one that may one day have the same dimensions as the asbestos scandal or the long-lasting litigation against big tobacco companies in the US, I have become used to personal defamation and numerous attempts to discredit me and my work. On several occasions I stated to my opponents: "I'm sorry, but for more than 50 years I have practised walking upright." Already, back in the mid-1990s, I had the unwanted privilege of proving that a major aircraft manufacturer even went so far as to make false statutory declarations in court in its silly attempt to hide an 'inconvenient truth' and prevent this from becoming public.

As a professional journalist I serve the public and I'm also used to, and obliged to, accept and reflect different opinions on a subject. What is amazing though in this very specific context is the fact that the aviation industry and responsible bodies in government and aviation authorities decline to comment or to answer my or my colleagues' questions at all. This has been the case with the manufacturers of aircraft and equipment and also the majority of the airlines we have been dealing with on this topic over the last years. Well, let's see where this will lead us to...

Nevertheless, I believe it is important that those who fall victim to this issue raise their voice, as Ms Beaumont is doing with this book, with her restless dedication to helping aircrews and passengers who have become affected as well. It is important that the public awareness is raised, as it can only be the combined efforts of public opinion that will initiate a long-overdue change in such a serious matter as this. This is a matter that has been one of the aviation industry's best kept secrets for almost 60 years and which may affect more generations, if not corrected now and within due time.

So please allow Bearnairdine Beaumont with this book to take you on to this flight; a journey that will give you an insider's view first hand and may be an eye-opener. And please have in mind that though you may not be affected to the same level as described here by those who suffer, one of your friends or loved ones may… From all that I learned from talking to and interviewing experts and scientists, the risk is very real for everybody who boards a plane, be it for business, leisure or just in faithfully serving an employer and doing one's job: care for and keep the souls aboard safe! Always happy landings.

Tim van Beveren

Aviator and Aviation Journalist

Berlin, March 2015

Part 1

Fly With Me

Take Off

April 1977

Spring was in the air as I walked down the right aisle of the huge Boeing 747 jumbo jet in my brand new dark-blue uniform dress and jacket, navy-blue high heels, the silver 'wing' and name badge with blue lettering pinned to the left lapel, and the yellow and blue striped scarf tied neatly around my neck. My long, mahogany coloured hair was piled up on my head and pinned in to a 'banana', and my make-up was perfect. I looked, smiling, to the left and the right, pretending to be doing the pre-take-off seat belts check, just minutes before the passengers actually boarded flight 401 to New York.

I was so excited!

My very first flight and to the city of cities: New York!

Born to Fly

For once you have tasted flight you will walk the earth with your eyes turned skywards, for there you have been and there you will long to return.

(attributed to Leonardo da Vinci)

My parents had instilled the travelling bug in me. Dad was a passionate pilot who had financed his training from scratch himself, and started flying gliders at age eighteen, to finally receive his commercial pilot's licence in 1948 in England, six years later. Mum was an air hostess for a few years in the early 1950s, before I arrived exactly nine months after their wedding in 1953. They had met, very cliché, while both were employed at British European Airways. Dad proudly wore his uniform, as did his best man, and Mum was a beautiful black-haired bride, with a tiny waist, in a winter-white wedding dress and matching bolero jacket made from a heavy, flowing velvet material, carrying a bouquet of red and white roses with ivy wound through them. A beautiful January bride indeed with her two bridesmaids, her red-haired sister and her best friend, both in warm burgundy-red velvet.

Instead of flying all his life for the same airline, my father preferred to fly for various companies while Mum created a home in the country he was based in. So we got to live in Africa, India and Lebanon, Germany, England and Switzerland. Once, a few months before I was born, he was employed as a private pilot to a very wealthy Italian Count; but having to be on standby all the time twenty four hours a day, hardly getting to do any flying at all, he soon left that job in pursuit of his beloved career, adventures and to see the world. Later he was recruited by the Royal Air Force to fly evacuation flights out of war zones.

I had been working in my chosen profession in a doctor's surgery for several years, when at the age of 23 I gave in to my sense for adventure and to my father's constant, kindly prodding, and followed in his footsteps, but because pursuing a career as an airline pilot was not yet *en vogue* for women in Europe, I became a flight attendant, like my mother had been.

Upon Dad's recommendation I applied for a job with a well-known airline in the German-speaking part of Europe, which he told me was 'the best'.

The charming, smart and elegant ladies who interviewed me were two of the first stewardesses of this airline, and seemed delighted at my 'whole family' being aviators. Many years later one of the psychologists told me that he had not favoured my employment and upon my question why, said that he thought I might be a bit of a rebel, but he was luckily over-ruled by these ladies.

To be honest, he wasn't entirely wrong! But this was something that still lay well hidden within me and something I would discover only thousands and thousands of air miles later.

Then and there I was looking forward to my new life. My parents were happy and Dad, especially, was proud of me. From then on he followed every 'routing' and logged the coordinates of my flights; he flew with me on paper to the various locations he too had visited.

Fasten Your Seat Belts and Fly Away With Me

The past, present, and future colourfully mingle and pull us here, there and everywhere.

(Bearnairdine Beaumont)

In the 1970s flying was... like we were on the stage. It still had glamour to it and most girls looked very elegant and were very proud to be air hostesses. High-heeled, we gracefully and smilingly swanned through airports, heads held high, beauty-case (not flight kit) in one gloved hand; the suitcase, without wheels at that time, followed on a trolley that one of the pilots, or other gentlemanly crew member, was pushing.

There were china plates, crystal glasses, and coffee pots and cutlery made of silver. Air hostesses were regarded with envy and admiration by those who stayed on the ground and with respect by passengers. Our airline paid us well and had us staying in four and five star hotels worldwide. Sometimes we were greeted with a cocktail or a Baccara rose as a welcome gesture from the hotel management – that's how much they valued us and the business they got through our airline!

And it was romantic.

It was the romance of the skies. You could take off and be in another world.

For the first few years I flew on Boeing 747 jumbo jets and the somewhat smaller Boeing 707 – long-haul trips only, which took me away from my small flat I now called home from five days, up to twenty-one on an Australia rotation.

Being a sun lover I enjoyed the possibility of following the sun around our wonderful planet; to soak up some hot sunshine in exotic places while winter was in full swing at home, and all while 'on duty' was just fantastic. I regarded that as a real treat and a bonus; who else could say of their job that it was like being on holidays a lot of the time?

On many layover days in those exotic places, while waiting for the return flights, I didn't only hang out at the luxurious hotel pools where we were accommodated, nor only went shopping, but I toured. On my own or with other crew members I went to see famous monuments and many of nature's beautiful sights; I strolled through the markets and the colourful bazaars and spent hours in small shops that were selling bric-a-brac and antiques.

I loved the display of gorgeous, brightly-coloured materials. Splashes of colour, silks and brocades interwoven with silver or golden threads, from which African robes, Indian sarees, kimono and other traditional indigenous clothing were tailored, which always have made women look like beautiful flower bouquets.

I enjoyed the interaction and the haggling for better prices for endless yards of beautiful silks. The family of the vendor grew bigger and bigger, and he theatrically threw his hands in the air in exasperation. He asked me and the space around us, how I thought he should feed so many mouths if he gave me such a low price? "Memsahib, me and my children will starve but for you my friend, take it, take it at this exceptionally good, very low price!" And I walked away with a bag full of beautiful silks and him calling after me: "Come again Madame, welcome, welcome", with a big smile on his brown face, black eyes twinkling, both of us happy, and both of us knowing he had still made a good profit.

Oh, and the delicious fruit, a lot of which one could not yet find in Europe, or only at exorbitant prices. I always took a huge basket back home, filled with pineapples, avocados, mangoes, papayas, coconuts – you name it. Or I brought oriental spices and herbs for cooking, meat from Argentina, Idaho potatoes and sour cream from America. Armfuls of beautiful orchids from Bangkok and artwork from Africa. From India wood carvings, from Japan silk paintings and jade and real cashmere jumpers from China; even an antique table and six matching chairs from Portobello Road in London, all of which were stacked in a nearly empty first class compartment.

Around The World in More Than 80 Days

Happiness is like a butterfly which when pursued is just beyond your grasp, but which if you sit down quietly may alight upon you.

(Nathaniel Hawthorne)

Nairobi was definitely a huge favourite; I requested this flight rotation on a nearly monthly basis. Perhaps I loved Africa so much because we used to live there. I went on many safaris; one particularly stuck in my memory. The safari guide, who, remembering it later on, somehow reminded me of Sean Connery as Allan Quatermain in the movie *The League of Extraordinary Gentlemen*, had picked us up. We were staying at a lovely lodge superbly situated in the lee of Mount Kilimanjaro and sheltered by the volcanic splendour of the Chyulu Hills and, as it seemed, in the middle of nowhere.

One night a buzzer alerting us to wildlife approaching woke us. Looking out of my window I was practically eye-to-eye with a magnificent elephant that had come for a drink at the water hole. He seemed to be staring at me, lightly flapping his ears, his huge tusks nearly touching the floor.

We were ushered via a loud whisper coming from the loud speaker in the wall of each room, to the thatched central dining area with its rock-built bar and a viewing terrace looking directly on to the water hole. One by one, but also in small groups, the beautiful beasts of Africa appeared. A mother rhino came with her baby, who playfully slid on his bottom down the bank to the water hole, and then, on its short, wee, stumpy legs, hurried back up again for more of the fun, while mother looked on; I could have sworn she was smiling. Hyenas came slouching in their weird hunched, submissive-looking manner out of the bushes, cautious of the bigger animals.

And then I felt something like a whisper on my arm. Thinking someone had touched me, I looked, I gasped and everybody turned to see why. A gorgeous silvery blue, very big butterfly had landed out of nowhere on my lower arm. They told me its name was 'Blue Beauty' and it sat there daintily cleaning itself... I hardly dared to breathe! What an amazing moment – it stayed there for many minutes, transforming me into a butterfly lover for life. Butterflies appeared thereafter throughout my life in the weirdest moments and oddest places, alive or as symbols.

In Amboseli National Park I became very close with two cheetahs who had been brought in to the caretaker, after they were found injured. They were now ready to be let go again. I was allowed to enter their cage – which had to be the experience of a lifetime. The male came up to me, circled me, sniffed my jeans, then stood beside me and allowed me to stroke him, purring loudly. Enjoying it, he leaned against my legs, while the female stood close by, watching and not sure what to do. A friend, who stayed on the other side of the fence mind you, took pictures, which I still treasure!

A Passage to India

Ah yes Bombay! Give me a place anywhere else in the world that is such an assault to the senses already at the airport! The non-stop storm of car horns blaring, children asking for souvenirs like ballpoint pens and vendors everywhere you go; nothing can prepare the mind to this amount of noise, colours and smells. I delighted in the Indian food and their culture. The beautiful bursts of colour coming from piles of silks, sarees, Punjabis, cushion covers, scarves, shawls, table clothes and napkins always seduced my artistic mind into buying more each time I was there to decorate my home with an exotic flair. Tables laden with pots filled with the many colourful powders, which were used to dye materials, tempted me to try it myself.

The Taj Mahal was a must-see! The magnificent monument that stands at the heart of India, and melts one's own heart when listening to the love story of Shah Jahan and Mumtaz Mahal, is a work of art. An English poet, Sir Edwin Arnold, best described it as: "Not a piece of architecture, as other buildings are, but the proud passion of an emperor's love wrought in living stones." Sigh!

I treated myself to heavenly body and head massages straight after arrival in the hotel... which was pure bliss after a long stuffy-aired night flight! I became a fan of the ancient holistic natural medicine called Ayurveda and yoga, both of which later on became important parts in my life.

Something Invisible

Two years into flying long-haul flights, allergies, or so I thought, began annoying me. Itchy skin, irritated, red eyes, breathing problems and dry coughs kept bothering me always during and after many flights.

But I thought nothing of it; although irritating it wasn't too bad and the doctors said, after their usual patch test routine, that I had a few allergies to pollen, trees and some animals. I did? I never knew... after all I had lived with cats and dogs and I used to go riding. As a child I had even helped out on a neighbouring farm, raking the hay in summer and mucking out the stables in winter.

I was told that such allergies can appear out of the blue, and to best have a series of desensitisation shots. I asked the doctor, who was a specialist for allergies and skin problems, if it could have anything to do with the aerosol disinsectant sprays we had to spray on board before landing in some countries. He said he doubted it, since according to his information they were harmless and suggested again to have the desensitisation shots done. So, I did that, three years in a row, from January to April, but they didn't seem to have the desired effect, except that my arm got very sore, swollen and inflamed and I still had those 'allergic' reactions.

The China Connection

Flowers may bloom again, but a person never has the chance to be young again.
So don't waste your time.

(Chinese proverb)

I was on the second flight my airline undertook to Beijing – it was winter and Christmas; we had a seven day layover.

We rented bicycles to get around the city, since at that time there weren't many cars around and certainly none to hire. Old Beijing was wonderful and amazing: those narrow lanes twisting through older sections formed an open-air museum, where one could happily cycle or wander around aimlessly for hours. We usually returned to the hotel with black smudges all over our faces, only white circles around the eyes where the sunglasses had offered protection. Our clothes were covered in soot, which was very dense in the air, especially in those ancient parts of the city where everybody was heating with coal. The air was clogged with dirt, making it hard to breathe at times.

One day, I had just descended from the Great Wall; I came across an elderly Chinese man who was sitting cross-legged on a cushion at the foot of the steps, his long white hair in a plait and a moustache coming down in long feathery wisps alongside his mouth, framing his friendly smile. Beside him lay a pile of paper, each sheet rolled up like scrolls of ancient times, several pots of paint and his special Chinese painting brushes of all sizes.

He was creating lovely paintings, pictures of branches with blossoms, with birds or butterflies sitting on them or flying around them. I watched him for a while when the others called me to hurry up, our bus was ready to leave.

As I was walking away he spoke, beaming his smile up at me and of course in Chinese said: "Wait, wait." Brushes flying over the long sheet of paper, he skilfully created in just a few minutes a beautiful picture – a branch, two butterflies and dark red blossoms. He signed it, rolled it up and handed it to me. Surprised, I indicated how much I should pay him. He gestured: "No, no." He tried to tell me why: he pointed to his eyes and my eyes, and placed his hand on his heart... how very sweet of him!

Over the years I learned not to be shy about the many admiring comments I got regarding my eyes. They are an unusual colour, grey-green with a dark rim and for Chinese people then a rarity, or even a novelty. They often took me by surprise by coming up close, and I mean close, to stare in to my eyes; others asked me if I wore coloured contact lenses.

The next day another exchange between an elderly Chinese person, this time a woman, and me occurred. Two cyclists, one coming at full speed from the right, the other from the left knocked me down while I was cycling to the Forbidden City and its Palace Museum, to pick up a piece I had ordered at the little jade shop. I felt slightly off balance when I arrived and felt fairly pale, which was noticed by the shop owner who brought me a chair. I sat down and rolled up my trouser leg to inspect the wound. He saw it, went to the back room and returned with his mother. She was dressed in the old Chinese style, her long, nearly pure white hair in a plait down her back reaching her waist. She inspected my leg, which was still bleeding, said something and went out.

She came back a few minutes later carrying a bowl of steaming water and some strips of linen, and proceeded to clean the wound. Then, taking some very suspicious looking green-black, rather smelly paste from another small bowl, she smeared it all over the wound, and then bandaged my shin with clean bits of material. She hand-signed, pointing at the old clock ticking on the wall, to leave it on for twenty-four hours, and waddled off.

It was amazing. The painful throbbing stopped within a few minutes and when I took the bandage off twenty-four hours later, healing had set in without any signs of infection, and there was no swelling or pain left! I still wonder what was in that paste.

It was my first experience with traditional Chinese medicine.

Surprise in the Land of the Rising Sun

If you do not enter the tiger's cave,
you will not catch its cub.

(Japanese proverb)

What fascinated me about Japan was their unity with nature. In everything – food, house décor, the kimono, ikebana and bonsai. Everything is so One with the seasons, and the seasons are so beautiful. I had to see the cherry blossoms and the plan was to head in the direction of Kawazu, home to a special variety of cherry blossoms. The Kawazu River, which flows through the centre of the town, is lined with cherry blossoms for about four kilometres. So on one layover all of us took off from Tokyo towards Kawazu by train. Boy, what an experience. Have you tried to get on a train in Japan? You have to move fast!

The train pulls in; doors open, people virtually spill out of the carriages shoulder to shoulder and rush off to wherever they are going. Just as the last ten or so step out, everybody waiting pushes in at the same time... hurry, hurry... don't be too polite or you will be left behind... which happened to me; just as I was wanting to step into the already crowded carriage, the doors hissed shut... and the train left with my crew waving and laughing behind the windows, gesturing for me to wait there. Very funny indeed! For once I had followed the leader of the pack and didn't have directions with me, and at that time hardly any signage was in English at train stations, certainly not there. So I stood there, looking a bit dumbfounded.

Half an hour later they came back for me... this time I managed to get into the train, and about two hours later we had a wonderful day viewing the cherry blossoms.

I admired the Japanese politeness when greeting and thanking. Also the fabulous creative way of wrapping up anything you bought was amazing. The kimono fascinated me. The beautiful silks and brocades were neatly stacked and kimonos with fantastic dyes, even hand paintings, showing whole stories or landscapes, or a pattern with butterflies or cherry blossoms for a spring kimono, or bamboo, plum blossoms and pine trees for winter, were hung accurately on display. It is a complete work of art, as is getting dressed in one. The twelve or more separate pieces that are worn, matched, and secured in prescribed ways, definitely require the assistance of a licenced kimono dresser.

Of course I had to try the bathhouse! It was a learning experience, starting with taking the proper entrance, which was indicated in the colour of the 'noren', hanging curtains, red for female and blue for male. Bathers were naked. We were used to 'no swim suits allowed' since in our part of the world going naked into a sauna was nothing new. One brought small towels that were used to cover private parts when outside of the baths, which I found very polite. After pre-washing body and hair I stepped into the water. WOW, it was hot... slowly, slowly slide in, sit, and don't move. The wee towel landed on my head, which seemed handiest and others demonstrated to do. Relaxing quietly with everybody respecting the others' space was very enjoyable, and the feeling of utter cleanliness afterwards was wonderful.

And in Japan it was where another one of those 'once in a lifetime' experiences happened. It was an invitation by a stranger whom, tired as I was, I first didn't recognise. He stood beside me at the Osaka hotel reception after arrival from Anchorage. I thought he was some guy trying to chat me up, and hardly looked at him. He asked me what I was doing that evening, to which I answered slightly annoyed at being bothered that I was just going out with my friends for dinner.

Then, just like that and with a wide smile he invited me 'and your friends' to 'my concert this evening'. His concert? Suddenly I was wide-awake and actually looked at the man and recognised who was extending that invitation – Carlos Santana himself!

What a blast, best seats, back stage passes and the road manager were waiting for us a few hours later. All tiredness was blown away! It was the most orderly concert I have ever been to. The

Japanese audience was, even in their excitement, very disciplined. After the concert we met the band for a drink and some food. I will never really know why Carlos chose to invite me.

I met many lovely stars and other celebrities as the years went by. Sir Peter Ustinov was a particularly delightful gentleman, as was Sir Ben Kingsley; the chat with Joe Cocker was fun and Arnold Schwarzenegger, Engelbert Humperdinck, Jethro Tull, 007's 'Q', Desmond Llewelyn who was joking all the time, and many more, were the nicest of passengers and so unassuming.

Breathing Difficulties

The time came when I started making the connection between the spraying of the disinsectant sprays and my coughing, sneezing and itchy, red eyes. I sometimes was also short of breath and wheezy directly after spraying. One inevitably inhaled some of the mist sprayed overhead of the passengers, which then rained down softly onto their heads, before landing in Australia, South Africa and many other places. This was done to kill any mosquitoes and other bugs that could bring unwanted illnesses, like malaria, into these countries. We had to spray and empty six to eight cans of this insect-killer, of which we were told was harmless for humans. These had to then be presented to the health officer who boarded the plane, closing the door behind himself again, and who would then check the aircraft and the empty cans, before allowing disembarkation.

I began feeling nauseated when filling my car with petrol, and had to cover my nose to avoid inhaling the rising fumes. My husband made fun of me, telling me how nice it smelled, and he took deep breaths to demonstrate it. My chest got tight and I often gasped for breath, coughing violently, when I accidentally inhaled a 'mouthful' of perfume or paint. My mouth and throat went instantly bone dry and swollen. I didn't seem to be able to tolerate any fragranced products, such as cleaning products, laundry detergents and fabric softeners, never mind my perfumes.

Showering or taking a bath was becoming an ordeal. My skin started to itch like I had hundreds of ants under my skin, and red, angry-looking flares appeared, along with outbreaks looking like measles all over my body. My legs were worst, and no amount of scratching until the skin was raw and bleeding, nor applying of ointments, stopped it. I couldn't figure out if it was from the water, or from the shower gel or from the detergents in the towels. I couldn't use pools either; the chlorine in the water in contact with my skin and the smell of it had the same effect, so I quit swimming.

Before long my asthma attacks increased and got so bad that my physicians, now two of them, gave me prescriptions for an inhaler and anti-histamine medication, together with the diagnosis: adult onset of bronchial asthma, probably induced by allergies. I was told to stay home for three weeks. Again I mentioned that I seemed to have the problem on board and mainly when we had to spray those insecticide sprays before landing – but still they didn't make a connection, assuring me of the harmlessness of those sprays.

I went on my next flights thinking I must have an allergy problem and possibly some kind of flu then, and since it had eased off after the sick leave and I also didn't feel so completely exhausted any more, I thought all was fine.

Jet-lag in Alaska

Perhaps they are not stars, but rather openings in heaven where the love of our lost ones pours through and shines down upon us to let us know they are happy.

(Author unknown)

The night skies in Alaska, covered with trillions of twinkling stars, were so beautiful! Ah yes, Anchorage! Because of the two time zones, with an eighteen-hour time difference, which we crossed on our way to Japan and back, we had, instead of a hotel room, a small apartment each. This way we could cook our meals in our own time, and do some washing due to the length of the rotation. Such activities happened sometimes wide-awake at 2am, which was for our personal body clocks the middle of the day before or after!

We had two station cars, which we were allowed to use to get around with for grocery shopping and excursions to distant mountains and rivers, to go on nature trails and salmon fishing. We usually ended up having BBQ parties in the beautiful wilderness, or back in our apartment block in the crew lounge, where sometimes, just sometimes, the parties got slightly out of hand.

On the way back from an outing in the wilderness we used to stop at the quirky Bird-House Tavern on the far side of Anchorage. Its walls were covered – literally covered, inches thick in some places, with business cards, bits and pieces of uniforms (one of our girls had left her yellow summer uniform dress hanging there), bras and other bits and pieces of clothing. The tilted wooden floor was always thick with sawdust or peanut shells, and people were packed elbow to elbow in the tiny establishment. The bar was so slanted you had to keep your hand on your beer mug to keep it from sliding down the counter while the bartender pulled his pranks on unsuspecting customers, looking innocent as could be, to then crack up with laughter when we all fell for them.

Lots of fun memories! Sometimes the job felt so good, I couldn't wait to go on the next flight, forgetting completely about headaches, itchy skin and red eyes.

Body Alarm

In 1982, after an Osaka to Anchorage flight, I arrived home with severe palpitations, headache, and massive tremor in numb, but at the same time, tingling hands, fluttering eye lids, and a feeling of utter distress. The airline medic, who was my first port of call, thought I was having a jet-lag issue, and told me to go home and rest for a few days.

Two or three days later my heart was still racing, my pulse was constantly at around 125 beats per minute. I hardly slept at night and felt very hot all the time. I lost weight rapidly, although I was eating and always hungry, and I was very edgy. I finally visited my physician who diagnosed a hyperactive thyroid gland just by the symptoms I showed, but she also followed up with the relevant blood tests to confirm. All levels were way too high. She thought that this could have happened due to jet-lag and way too many long-haul and night flights, and again prescribed a two week sick leave. I told her that sometimes I coughed more after using the inhaler, so she changed the prescription, assuming that I was reacting to some ingredient. I had stopped smoking long ago, so that wasn't the problem. She was confused and decided we would monitor this for a while and see.

I had to take medication for the thyroid to rebalance it, which helped. Not a thought was given by anyone of the possibility that toxic compounds I might be in contact with, that can disrupt the endocrine system (US National Library of Medicine[1]), could be a reason, although such facts were already well documented.

In the years that followed I learned that one sometimes has to (gently) guide the physicians in the right direction but, of course, to do that one has to have at least some basic knowledge and information in toxicology oneself, which at the time I did not.

The Russia House with Love from Hong Kong

All we can know is that we know nothing.
And that's the height of human wisdom.

(Leo Tolstoy, War and Peace)

I only ever had one Hong Kong flight. But on that one flight I was very lucky: I got to see the famous Russian Bolshoi Ballet dancing *Giselle*. A first class passenger was unable to attend and gave his tickets to a colleague and me, who had looked after him and his wife during the flight. More or less in passing by while we were waiting for our luggage, he handed them over and said, "Enjoy, we can't go", and walked away.

That was such a treat. In Moscow, where I had wanted to see the show a couple of months earlier, I had missed them. The reason being: they were on world tour. So I had finally caught up with them.

Instead, when I was in Moscow I had an adventure of a different kind.

While wandering through the Pushkin Arts Museum I backed away from a painting to view it from afar and bumped into a couple, nearly toppling the three of us over. We laughed aloud while going "Shhh, shhh" at the same time, pointing out that we shouldn't make so much noise. We introduced ourselves and made it clear that neither they nor I were masters of the other's language. But I ended up with an invitation to coffee and cake and then they took me on a tour to other sites in the city in areas tourists do not usually get to see.

The next evening they picked me up at the hotel by car. I had to wait outside because they were not allowed in. We arrived, after a ten minute drive, in a dark looking, not well-lit street lined by high poplar trees and rows of several storey high houses on each side.

Ivan parked his Lada and we crossed the street, heading toward a sapphire blue door. No signs or lights, other than one shining down from above the door. There was a butterfly on a sign indicating the name, I assumed, of the establishment.

I had a slightly funny feeling in my tummy by now, but a surprise awaited me. Entering through the blue door we climbed up narrow stairs. Light streamed out of rooms on each small floor, and laughter and people talking could be heard. Each floor had one dining room with only a couple of tables where diners were enjoying their meals. We reached the top floor. This room was a lot bigger and had a fantastic view over Moscow. The tables were beautifully set. Starched white linen with embroidered rims spread across the tables, silver cutlery, glistening crystal glasses, laden with caviar and blinees, borsch and kasha, which we enjoyed immensely while telling each other about our lives.

The very tasty meal was followed by delicious desserts: a choice of khalva or apricot cream or both as Ivan and Katjenka indicated, and insisted I try both; followed by coffee, vodka, cognac and Krim champagne. There was beautiful background music being played by three students; a gorgeous Gipsy woman, thick black locks reaching her waist, in colourful long skirts and a lacy, shoulder-free blouse, sang soulful Russian songs, black eyes sometimes glistening with passionate tears.

We talked lots and resorted to drawing on napkins and thumbing through my dictionary I had brought, to help explain what we were saying. They were telling me about their dacha (a little country abode many city people had), which I was invited to visit; they were such friendly hospitable people, who left me back at the hotel late that night, inviting me to come 'another time' with them to Odessa. It was one of my best nights out.

Gold Fingers

In Dubai and Abu Dhabi we went wild buying gold jewellery at the day's gold price. They only weighed the piece and that was what one paid, which made it very reasonable. All the girls who flew Boeing 707s were recognisable because, I swear, we looked like Christmas trees. We wore at least three, if not more, gold chains and thick necklaces, several chains and bracelets on very tanned wrists and ankles, and rings on more than one finger of each hand.

Forget about the 'not allowed with uniform' regulations, we were the elite crew and we took liberties and were given some leeway. Only a few hundred of us were high enough in seniority and had the privilege to fly the old lady Boeing 707 in the '70s to mid-'80s. Envied by everybody else, we benefited from the wonderful locations allocated to Boeing 707, most of them with long layovers, plus long rest-time after the flight at home. That was still the era when flight operations was generous and minimum rest times were often extended by many hours, even a day or two.

Of course there was the more sombre Kuwait or even Jeddah stopovers where we had to sit apart from the male crew, separated by a fence in the restaurant. We had to make sure, when we went out, to wear long kaftans or similar all-covering clothes. Not to mention the naughty things we did, such as preparing 'after-burner' orange juices just before landing, to take with us. It was forbidden to bring alcoholic drinks in to the country… so we invented ways around that!

Smelly Socks

When we came on board an aircraft, especially after it had arrived from a long-haul flight, most of us noticed a stuffy, weird, sometimes mouldy smell comparable to a wet dog, or sweaty sock smells as if a whole gym had been on board, and other unpleasant smells, such as vomit. We never knew what it was, wrinkled our noses, commented on it, and sometimes sprayed our own expensive perfumes to cover it up and just got on with our job.

In time I became aware that my uniform smelled awful after flights, so much so I couldn't bear it! After each flight it had to be hand-washed. Dry cleaning had become impossible since I had noticed that the smell from the dry cleaners caused me sneezing and skin reactions. The horrible musty smell wasn't removed by dry cleaning anyway; on the contrary, it seemed to increase it. I suddenly had a persistent ringing in my ears. Headaches had become my constant companion, which was unusual for me, and the wheezing and full blown asthma attacks, gasping for breath, were becoming more frequent; only easing when I had several days off between flights.

Allergies to all kinds of things began manifesting as the list grew longer and longer, accompanied in time not only by sneezing, red eyes and sinusitis, but nose bleeds and terribly itchy skin, balance problems and dizziness. I was also developing a sensitive digestion, which was most annoying. I had always been proud of a digestion and stomach as 'strong as a horse's', but that dramatically changed. The swollen 'Boeing-baby-belly' never ceased and certain foods caused severe IBS symptoms.

When I drank wine, my skin flared up into an angry-looking red-hot and itchy blotch just above my chest and up my throat. Sometimes the inside of my nose went bone dry and swelled up and I had to breathe through my mouth; my lungs also reacted, with dry coughing, and the now well-known wheezing, which came with sounds of squeaking, was very disturbing. I used to laugh it off and said that I was a great indicator for cheap wines[2]. Little did I know what I was indicating!

It usually took a day or more for these reactions to calm down.

One day I nearly suffocated after just finishing a kiwi fruit. My tongue and throat went dry, swelled up within seconds and I could scarcely breathe – I was terrified I was going to suffocate and I tried hard not to panic. I was brought to ER where they gave me anti-histamines and a saline drip. I was diagnosed with a sulphites and mould fungus allergy, which explained, as I was told, the reactions to wine. But what caused my reaction to the kiwi no one could tell me.

Very much later I learned that vine-growing kiwis, like grapes, are heavily sprayed with pesticides and fungicides[3].

Heaven on Earth

Mauritius was made first, and then heaven and that heaven was copied after Mauritius.

(Mark Twain)

Oh, the five-day layovers in Mauritius which once turned into a ten-day holiday. The message had just arrived when I joined the crew at the breakfast buffet, smart in uniform and ready for pick-up.

Our captain came back from reception, a serious look on his face. He told us that due to a bird strike, our plane was stuck in Nairobi waiting for a new engine and there was no replacement. And that he was very sorry, but we had to stay another four or five days. By now grinning widely of course. Shrieks of delight, and up to the rooms we shot, firing our uniforms into the corner, hopping back into those itsy-bitsy bikinis, slinging a colourful pareo low around our hips, grabbing the sun tan lotion and back down at the beautiful white beach we were, in ten minutes flat! So much fun, wind surfing, lazing in the sun with delicious cocktails, buying yet another pareo to wear from one of the beach vendors and skinny dipping at midnight in the light of a huge full moon! We had evenings out eating the delicious local foods in lovely, open-air restaurants in balmy air, and during the days there was the to-do list of viewing the beautiful sights such as Trou de Cerfs and the amazing Seven Coloured Earths of Mauritius. That was the life!

Eventually the day of departure came. On that flight back we returned via Khartoum not Nairobi, which was in a way a special treat for me. Khartoum was the city where we lived for several years in the mid-1950s, when Dad flew for Sudan Airways. We had a lovely bungalow on the outskirts of the city, and many memories came flooding back from that time.

But another flight to Mauritius was not so heavenly. After spraying the cans of pesticides half an hour before landing I walked back up the aisle to the first class galley and was already coughing that dry cough as if something had got stuck in my chest and I was having problems breathing. A headache was building and I felt dizzy. It had to be from that stuff, I thought. I used my inhaler several times until it helped a bit. On the way to the hotel I was wheezing more and feeling very sick and extremely tired, so much so I fell asleep in the bus and my colleagues had to wake me upon arrival at the hotel. I was feeling weak, very weak, and my brain was in a fog.

Most of the time on that layover I lay in bed feeling miserable; the physician who was assigned by our company for crew health issues en route was called, but not available, so I told the purser I'd try and sleep it off.

After hours of sleeping and waking without feeling rested, I stared in horror at my pillow, which was literally covered with hair that had fallen out overnight.

A study published in 2012 documents that flight attendants on commercial aircraft disinsected with pyrethoid insecticides are exposed to pesticides (organophosates) at levels that result in elevated toxicity burden and internal accumulation which is comparable to pesticide applicators. So logically it can be expected that passengers would be similarly exposed to pesticides on those flights.[4]

List of Countries Requiring Disinsection[5]

Aircraft disinsection is the use of insecticides on some international flights to kill possible insects that might carry, say, malaria, that can be brought on board in the luggage or are blown in by air (wind). This spraying of neurotoxic agents, which can kill bugs within seconds, was first used in the 1930s but it is being reduced because of the effects on passengers and crew. Some of the countries that require spraying are Australia, Barbados, France, Indonesia, Mauritius, New Zealand, South Africa, Switzerland and the United Kingdom.

Please be aware that, if you are a frequent flyer, you are also very much in danger of developing health problems; perhaps now you can even make a connection between symptoms you have experienced and a flight? Even if you fly rarely, but are susceptible due to your genetic print (but who knows that before a flight, or at all?), you can also be in danger of falling ill due to the spraying, and of course the other contaminants in the air you breathe in this enclosed tin with re-circulating air, the aircraft.

Trips Down other Memory Lanes

I now know, by an almost fatalistic conformity with the facts that my destiny is to travel...

(Ernesto 'Che' Guevara)

Being an avid reader and book collector all my life I went book hunting wherever I was. One time I was in Santiago de Chile with a colleague who was an antiques dealer in his spare time. We searched through shops in the ancient parts of the city where a collection of antiques stores could be found, clustered around Malaquias Concha and Caupolican. We dug for ages in piles of dusty old books, finding some lovely ones, even really old pieces, which later stood on my bookshelves.

Rio de Janeiro, although many layovers were fantastic – one memory was unpleasant; that's where we experienced a very sad situation. One of our girls would not listen to reason and wore her jewellery, although we told her it could be tempting and dangerous. We were going for dinner in the city, a good restaurant, but still, one never knew. We always tucked money into our shoes, left jewellery at the hotel and didn't dress too chic.

After dinner, we stood outside waiting for taxies, when a couple of lads walked by. Everything happened in split seconds. One of them ripped the girl's chains off her neck, she screamed, they ran, and our co-pilot, reacting to the situation without thinking, gave chase... they injured him badly with a knife, and got away anyway.

We brought him to ER, got him looked after and made sure he was ok. He deadheaded back with us. And so ended an otherwise pleasant trip...

Old Constantinople and 007

A bird will not fly with one wing.

(Turkish proverb)

I was in Istanbul a lot. Of course I visited the atmospheric and cavernous underground Basilica Cistern, famously used as a backdrop in the James Bond movie *From Russia with Love*. The 6th Century cistern providing a fresh water supply for buildings including the Emperor's palace was amazing.

The famous Hagia Sophia, with its great architectural beauty, was so impressive with its beautiful mosaic artwork and paintings with the many striking blues, a colour I love, was a pleasure to the eye.

I sneezed a lot and my sinuses were stuffy after visiting these buildings. I had indeed become very sensitive to mould, which can be found everywhere, but especially in old buildings, damp areas and even air-conditioning. Aircraft air-conditioning.

One time I visited the Istanbul Hammam, which was an experience in itself! Naked, only a towel slung around my hips, I was told to pour warm water over myself using a copper bowl, which I filled and refilled over and over again, from a tap in the marble wall, for about fifteen minutes. Then the bath lady decided I was pre-washed enough and indicated for me to come along and lie on a marble slab next to the pool upon which she took out a bath brush, which looked very much like a floor scrubbing brush, and a slab of green soap. She worked up a lather and commenced to scrub me from head to toe – I thought my skin would come off or that I would react to the soap, but no! It was fabulous; she scrubbed for ages and didn't leave out an inch. Obviously the old fashioned soap had no chemicals in it.

Then I was rubbed dry with a not very soft towel after which my skin was warm and tingling. I was escorted to a tiny relaxation chamber where I was rather sternly ordered to relax at least half an hour, but before that she generously applied lovely smelling rose oil all over me and massaged my back and shoulders firmly. Then she brought me a small glass of hot, very sweet peppermint tea and left me to sleep, which I did. I nearly missed the time to go and meet the crew for dinner, I was blissfully relaxed. I was truly enjoying my profession.

History Trails

Certainly, travel is more than the seeing of sights; it is a change that goes on, deep and permanent, in the ideas of living.

(Mary Ritter Beard)

Let me not forget to mention some of the beautiful European cities. I used to walk miles and miles, sightseeing through ancient parts of the towns, into churches, museums, palaces and castles, tracing footsteps of famous authors or actors in just as famous cafés in Vienna, Budapest, Paris or Rome.

A lot of the romance I mentioned came easily to life in the Viennese coffee houses where I would linger for hours with a book, drinking several of the special Viennese coffee combinations and eating delicious sweet pastries and rich cakes.

Or Paris! Taking a walk to the artistic neighbourhood of Montmartre and admiring the many artists working away in the sunshine, then sitting outside in one of the many sidewalk bistros was one of my favourite pastimes. Of course, to go and dig for old books in the Shakespeare and Company bookstore in the Rue de la Bùcherie and lose hours doing so, was a must. After visiting one of the many beautiful monuments I loved to take an evening stroll to the River Seine and cross one of the bridges down which one could meander and admire the beautifully lit up sights of the city. On many of these trips I was in the company of my special someone, and the pleasure of being able to enjoy such romantic excursions together was to be forever embedded in my memory.

London, Barcelona, Madrid, Hamburg, Munich, Brussels, Amsterdam, Venice... ah Venice!

Such a magical place with its Murano glass and beautiful carnevale masks and the romantic gondoliers. So many antique places to visit in all those little narrow streets, up and down tiny, well-trodden stairways and across the famous bridges. Venice had this romantic flair about it. Once when I was there, Venice shimmered in its summer haze like the most impressionist work done by any artist, and was a sight to behold.

Being exposed to the heat and humidity accompanied by some slightly pungent backwaters was a small price to pay; the pleasure of viewing Venice's churches and museums, which offered hours of antique glories, were well worth it. I was there one time in February when the Carnevale was in full swing. What a sight!

Gorgeous masks, people dressed up beautifully, stood on display leaning in striking poses against the pillars on St Mark's Square, or sitting at café tables. Or walking across the plaza, some prancing delicately like peacocks showing off their colourful fantasy costumes!

Some artists alongside the road offered face painting and created a beautiful feather and flowers design across my forehead, left eye and cheek in blues and greens, it looked fantastic!

The Americas

What is life? It is the flash of a firefly in the night. It is the breath of a buffalo in the wintertime. It is the little shadow, which runs across the grass and loses itself in the sunset.

(Crowfoot, Blackfoot Warrior)

And of course, apart from Alaska, the other states of America, or should I say particular cities – Chicago, New York, Boston, San Francisco, Los Angeles, Philadelphia, Washington and Dallas. My favourite was Boston. I never managed to travel far outside of most cities, other than to Sacramento, to the beautiful impressive redwoods and the lovely Lake Tahoe, due to short layovers, but I did visit many of the sights in them.

Yes, I loved the job and made a career – I advanced first to purser, followed by flight attendant instructor, then check purser, which meant as much as inflight supervision; we were not integrated in the crew but wrote reports, watching the crew members perform their duties with eagle eyes, anything from safety briefing, to correctly observed emergency procedures and regulations, politeness and friendliness toward our passengers, their teamwork abilities and so on over several days; we also had office hours and were required to take part in meetings with the management to brainstorm whatever needed brainstorming. We trained, checked and examined flight attendants and pursers alike, giving them their yearly on-the-job evaluation. We gave them tips and advice on how to improve their work and their other on-board duties if necessary or we gave commendations for particularly good work well done. Something I enjoyed immensely.

Little did I know how detrimental to my health the decision to continue flying, and making a career out of it, would become...

Behind Closed Doors

The years went by. I used my inhaler a lot and took anti-histamine tablets, plus the thyroid hormones and sometimes painkillers for the headaches. I wasn't sleeping well and felt terribly tired most of the time. The airline's policies had changed and our rest times were becoming shorter until they were down to 'minimum' rest time.

My sensitivity of smell had increased dramatically; so much so that I wasn't able to tolerate the fumes from those disinsectant sprays at all, plus many other smells. They made me feel so nauseous and within seconds I got the now well-known symptoms: headaches, red eyes and itchy skin, plus a feeling of dizziness and (hooray!) new symptoms: a feeling as if my brain was swollen and was applying pressure onto my left ear, causing hearing and balance problems.

Fragrances and scents from perfumes my colleagues were wearing started bothering me a lot. Many colleagues were also commenting in the meantime and to at least avoid the fumes from the disinsectant sprays we sometimes sprayed them empty outside of the aircraft doors before the passengers arrived. If that wasn't an option because some purser was abiding strictly by the rules, we sprayed them into the toilets, arm and shoulder, nothing else, reaching inside trying to keep the door closed as much as possible while emptying the cans.

Trying not to worry or become paranoid I just relied on the physicians' diagnoses – what could I do? At that time I still trusted fully in their wisdom and knowledge. And I continued flying. What a mistake.

My doctors advised me to take a long break. After more allergy testing, the list had again increased, my asthma was worse and the skin on my inner lower arms to the elbows never healed up. So I applied for a 'Kur', which is a form of health cure, in olden days called 'to take the waters' at specialised healthcare centres, a mix between clinics and hotels, which are located in well-known, approved and registered areas with unpolluted air, fresh water and generally healthy environment. After spending four weeks in a beautiful place in Bavaria, Germany, and under medical supervision, with special food and treatments, lots of fresh air and good water, I felt very much better.

It didn't last long.

Flashbacks

But I cannot forget.

In 1986 I went on one of the rare flights we requested, together with my husband. I became pregnant on that flight. I lost the baby after just passing the crucial three months, by three weeks. Since I had never expected it, I didn't notice the pregnancy. I didn't have any morning sickness or other obvious changes, so it went unnoticed that the tiny soul only lived for a short while and died as silently as she came, in me. When my body started rejecting the little dead body, it caused me horrible pain, but I thought I was just having a bad time of the month. Twice I went to a hospital's ER while en route on duty, and twice I was misdiagnosed and let go with strong pain killers; the doctor's relying on my "Not at all!" to their question, if I thought I could be pregnant.

Five days after my second ER visit I collapsed and was brought, blue lights flashing and sirens blaring to another hospital. After an emergency scan they told me that without a doubt I was pregnant and proceeded to prepare me for immediate surgery, there was no time to lose. Although I was barely able to focus, I was stunned and tried to relate to what they had told me, and feel something. I couldn't; then I was whisked away to the operating theatre. They saved my life in a four-hour, filled with complications as I was told later, operation. What I do remember is leaving my body at some stage, looking at myself from afar but at the same time into a space of blinding white light; I remember someone calling my name over and over again, the voice coming from very far away like an echo, others were shouting commands and it felt like I had a load of iron burning on my chest. Then the echoing voice became inaudible again, coming back a bit louder and I remember thinking 'Leave me alone!' while I was looking into the funnel of light. I reached for it, drifting in and out of life and consciousness. Then I heard someone ask: "Why are her eyes open? She is not focussing or hearing us – she's got beautiful eyes hasn't she?" I thought that was funny, and kept looking into that white light and drifted off again, leaving the voices behind. But then I started surfacing, reacting to the insistent echo of my name being called over and over, and I finally came to, my eyes suddenly saw again and a friendly voice behind a mask said in a relieved tone of voice, "Dear girl you gave us quite a fright, but everything is OK now!" while a soft hand stroked my cheek, and kind, smiling eyes above the mask looked into mine. I tried to smile back, but not knowing if I succeeded drifted off into a heavy sleep amid the clattering of instruments, just noticing the movement of the bed as I was wheeled off, then nothing.

When I slowly woke I looked into my husband's face. The first thing he said to me was: "Never ever look at me like that again." The look was of someone coming back to a place she did not want to be; a look of sadness and loss and no recognition. Over the following hours I noticed that the nurses seemed to be extra kind with me, and when the doctor came and told me what had happened and what they had to do, I understood why.

Later, when it began sinking in that I had been pregnant and had lost my little girl, never mind very nearly my own life, I tried to come to terms with it. My husband left me very much alone with my confusion and grief, telling me to get over it and get on with it. The near death experience returned in flashbacks regularly, not to haunt me but reminding me in a positive way of the sensation and clarity of images, which amaze me over and over again and the feeling of utter acceptance and peace of what is to come one day. Then, I felt weak, out of shape, unfit and tired, so very tired – and I had to force myself back into my life and to work.

I never got pregnant again. This too I put down to the organophosphate poisoning – they are toxins which contain endocrine disruptors[1] which have been, to mention just a few, linked to diabetes, thyroid problems (another one of my health issues as mentioned) and can cause infertility, miscarriages and development problems. For the record, nobody in my family ever had thyroid or fertility issues, diabetes or similar problems.

Many years later, when I lived in Ireland, I was finally able to connect with my little girl and let her go in a small ceremony which I held one day on a special, for me, sacred spot on the top of the hill on my land where I felt safe and able to bond with her wee soul. At long last I gave her her wings and told her: "Fly, fly my little One!" ...just as a beautiful big Red Admiral butterfly fluttered in circles around me, and danced off into the evening sunlight. I gave her the name Angel and planted a cherry tree on that spot, which showed off beautiful pink flowers every spring and attracted many butterflies.

Deterioration

My health was getting worse as time went on. Now I was sick regularly. I had flu-like colds, with very sore body pain accompanying them, sinusitis and bronchitis, which lasted very much longer than they normally would and asthmatic symptoms came along with them. The sudden onset of blasting headaches with an aching neck and the tinnitus never left me; I had concentration problems; I felt weak and couldn't do my fitness programme as usual. I noticed that my memory was becoming really bad. So bad, I couldn't remember people's names in my crew. Within minutes, even seconds after introduction I forgot them, and I had to check their name badges to remind myself, not even able to put names and faces together with the help of the crew name list.

The skin rashes hardly eased off nowadays. I was short of breath, wheezing and chronically tired, with black shadows around my eyes provoking unkind remarks from my husband who was used to me always looking glamorous. One day I came back from a flight with my face covered in a very sore, bone dry, flaky and itchy, angry-looking bright pink rash, especially around my eyes. It was so bad, the skin was cracking and I couldn't wear make-up. I had to cover it up with a pair of spectacles with slightly tinted glass. My hair was thinning and without its usual shine. I cut it short so it wouldn't look so bad. I got the hairdresser to perm it and add some highlights, and nearly choked on the fumes from those products! I had a massive headache after leaving the salon.

I couldn't not go to work, because exactly then I was in the middle of my training to become a training instructor.

Of course that didn't help, but still the guessing game was on about what was causing all these health problems. I used lotions and potions, prescribed and non-prescription ones, to feel better. But they made matters worse, and one product I was given for my hair reeked of tar, which caused me dizziness whenever I used it, so I didn't. I was given high doses of vitamin B12 in liquid form, which seemed to help a bit.

It went on and on. I became aware that somehow my marriage had become a manipulative and emotionally parasitic relationship. My husband became aggressive, aloof and hurtful, looking at me with distaste in his eyes. I was tossed in and out of mind games and together with everything else I felt like I was passing through the heavy load cycle in the washing machine. I tried talking with him but he didn't understand and lost patience. He became verbally nasty, and let not only his eyes roam elsewhere.

In the middle of all that, my beloved Dad died. He was only 63. He succumbed to cancer. His eyesight had become worse than ever, and he hardly recognised me when I visited him a few weeks before he passed. I knew, from the time he had to quit flying until the end, that he mourned the loss of his flying career, he had been a pilot with heart and soul. The health issues for his 'loss of licence on medical grounds' were symptoms I later recognised very well: double vision, tunnel vision, dizziness, headaches, allergies and sensitivities, weakness, chronic fatigue, concentration problems and no physician could find a reason.

When, years later, I was reading through his flight logs, I concluded that his health issues had begun shortly after he had started flying jets. They became progressively worse, forcing him to stop flying at the age of 48.

I learned much later that cancer is also very common in aviators, not only due to the high-level exposure to radiation, but also from the organophosphates then already entering the cabin via leaky seals, which contaminated the air; not to forget the aerosol pesticide spraying contributing to the chemical cocktail.

I was floored with grief at his early death.

One day, many years later, I visited his grave, which overlooked the beautiful Lake of Thun at the foot of the majestic Bernese Oberland Mountains of Switzerland. In the stillness of the afternoon, three air force jets appeared and, engines roaring deeply with reduced power, flew very low in a triangular formation exactly overhead of us. To my amazement the middle jet suddenly broke formation and rose upward to the skies... just like in a 'missing man' fly-by as if they were paying tribute to this pilot lying in his silent grave, on which we had placed a simple wooden cross engraved with a glider plane and his name. His last captain's cap decorated with the golden cords still hangs together with my coats in the porch.

Upheaval

In every living thing there is the desire for Love.

(D.H. Lawrence)

Not long after my Dad's funeral things went from bad to worse between my husband and me.

Phone calls began coming to the house, women asking for him and wanting to know who I was. One day he had the audacity to suggest that I meet one of them, saying: "She's really nice and she would like to meet you", adding the famous words: "There's nothing going on between us, we just had a good time." I couldn't stick it any longer. I had forgiven him many infidelities he didn't even know I knew about, but enough was enough with the added insult of his nasty behaviour. While he was on a long flight rotation I packed my belongings, found a tiny little flat in a private house owned by a lovely, very dear, deaf lady, who after her divorce rented out her second floor. There were two small apartments. Another young woman in the middle of a divorce rented, not long after, the other flat. The three of us got along 'like a house on fire', and helped each other with lots of humour through the difficult times.

A very unpleasant divorce one year later, during which my husband went completely berserk, and instead of apologising threatened to first shoot me, then the dog, then himself, freed me at last and gave me space to breathe. He tried to punish me by not allowing me to have Artus, our dog, a German Shepherd rescue from Spain. I loved this dog who had walked up one day to the small holiday home we owned. I will never forget the look on Artus' face and the way his ears had that sad hanging and at the same time begging, 'Please don't go' look when I left our house. He stood motionless, gazing at me through the gate as I stroked him and promised him, tears streaming down my face to see him as often as I could. It hurt me a lot.

For a while I had the impression that the man was stalking me and I found messages on my answering machine, with him trying to disguise his voice while snarling nasties into the phone or I saw his car parked in places he shouldn't have been. But I tried to remain calm and ignore it all. Slowly things went back to normal, although it was hard to avoid him at the airport, since he could easily check my roster, but after a few times he finally stopped being around crew check-in 'by chance' when I logged in for a flight.

The Thread

An invisible thread connects those who are destined to meet
Regardless of time, place and circumstance. The
Thread nay stretch or tangle but it will never break.

(Chinese saying)

During that time I fell in love with this tall, handsome, pilot. He wore his hair in a longish style and sported a well-groomed moustache under an attractively chiselled nose. His blue eyes sparkled with humour and a gentle masculinity. We became lovers the moment we set eyes on each other. From then on we kept meeting on flights nearly every month, as if fate had her hands in it and was bringing us together. Every time we met we continued where we had left off, until the time came we decided we wanted more. We requested as many flights together as possible, trying not to be indiscreet, which was fairly easy for us since he was a check captain and I was check purser and as such could place our flight requests as additional crew members without disrupting flight operations.

It was a wonderful year following that decision. How he made me laugh. He taught me that a man could honour a woman in many ways. He stood for me to be seated when I left or came to the table. He opened doors for me, guiding me in by the elbow. He listened without interrupting me and was able to agree to differ if we were of different opinion, which didn't happen often. We went shopping, and usually he would buy me a gift, a perfume perhaps or a silk scarf or leather gloves. Not shy he always held my hand in public; he had the habit of placing his hand on my neck beneath my hair when we were walking somewhere which made me feel safe, loved and cherished; a part of me responded to those gestures with a never before felt appreciation, aware of the beauty of the space and time I was in with him, wanting it to never end.

He spoiled me. He showered me with roses, even for my hotel room. He refused to allow me to 'go Dutch' and always invited me to our shared meals or small outings we would undertake wherever we were. We walked and cycled a lot. We went to so many romantic spots in Paris, Venice, Vienna and many other cities, but then it was romantic for us wherever we were. We took boat trips down the Seine, or on Austrian or German lakes, we danced in the rain, we danced in jazz bars, we played chess in the hotel lobby at 3am in the morning, we sat in roadside cafés in Paris, Milan and Rome, enjoying the hustle and bustle, drinking coffees and him enjoying his cigars; we laughed and forgot the world around us. His desire for me showed in so many small, sometimes hidden gestures. But he would also swoop me into his arms, kissing me with hot lips and a wild urgency in the middle of a busy street. Our nights were filled with passionate, yet tender lovemaking, his arms wrapped around me, holding me like I had never known before.

We tried to forget that there was a life each of us had apart from the precious hours with one another.

But it was over too soon, way too soon.

We had tentatively started thinking of spending our life together, when fate took an unexpected turn. Just when he had wrapped his mind around tackling a legal separation, and my divorce had gone through, his wife got very sick.

Some of the things I loved so much about him were his compassion and his sense of responsibility even though this was exactly what would separate us. I knew I had to let him go. He didn't ask me to do so, on the contrary, he didn't understand, he fought and held on to me... he came looking for me, he wrote me letters begging me to stay, asking me to give him time, and that everything would sort itself out. But I couldn't. I knew he would be caught up in his responsibility as a husband of a sick wife, no matter what the reason was that had caused a rift in their relationship and had separated them so much, long ago.

I knew. I also knew more, because I had heard from some of his colleagues that she was widely known to be a very demanding person even before she became so ill, and that there would be stress and worry and sadness. I felt I had to do the right thing, or what I thought was the right thing, but felt like a mistake. My wide-open passionate heart was torn to shreds, and I cried rivers of tears. I never knew there could be so much heartache and pain. I didn't eat, I couldn't sleep. The heavy, aching longing for him was tearing me apart. But I said no. At some stage he got very angry and so frustrated because of my constant noes; he finally gave up.

It was one of the hardest decisions I ever made; to do the exact opposite of my deepest desires – while Lady Fear in the background paced up and down throwing her hands in the air insisting on making me wonder if I had made a mistake, while I tried to counter with all the reasonable arguments to soothe my wounded, hurting heart and soul. I tried to create a distance between us. I packed up and left the little flat I had felt so comfortable in and moved to another city where the airline had another base. I requested change of fleet, retrained and now flew Airbuses. This way the chance of bumping into each other was minimal, since he flew Boeing 737s and from main base. I avoided requesting flights to places where we could meet accidentally, because they were destinations he would fly to with his fleet. I even started dating someone else, just to try and get over him, but it didn't help and I broke it off.

All went quiet for a while. I thought that time would heal this terrible aching wound but it never did, not fully. My next birthday came up. I found a card in my crew mailbox. He didn't write much but it said everything needed to bring forth all the old feelings like a tidal wave had hit me. His birthday was two weeks after mine, and I sent him a card too... no more, no less. Silence descended again and life continued while I fiercely tried to push his face in my mind aside and ignore my desires.

Then my system finally succumbed to the toxins and I became really sick. I was medically grounded for nine months and had to focus on my health.

Winds in Spaces

But let there be spaces in your togetherness and let the winds of the heavens dance between you.
Love one another but make not a bond of love:
let it rather be a moving sea between the shores of your souls.

(Khalil Gibran)

One beautiful spring day a couple of years later, just before starting the day in my little health farm practice, I rushed to pick up the ringing phone expecting a client's call, when my heart nearly stopped. Then it burst into a wild gallop when I heard that small, rumbling laugh coming from deep in his chest, and the voice I had missed for so long said, "Hi, it's me". I walked around all day with a big, happy smile on my face and a song in my heart.

He telephoned just once in a while and on my birthdays, but we never met. Hearing his sexy voice and deep, warm laughter on the phone made me very happy and I drew from my memory the warmth of his arms around me and his gentle, lingering kisses on my lips; the kisses along my hairline and the gentlest ones on my temple. That whisper of a butterfly kiss, which had so deeply, intimately, tenderly told me I was loved.

His wife was still very sick, but modern medicine was helping her and kept her illness from progressing further. He never said much about it, only when I asked, which I didn't too often, treasuring the few moments I had with him. He didn't ever complain, but I knew, and sometimes his voice was very strained. One day, many years later, now retired from flying in the meantime, he admitted that he felt very restricted, that every step he took was questioned, that he longed for some freedom, and that he never had a moment on his own. My heart went out to him.

I knew him as I knew myself; he just needed a bit of space. He had even given up his beloved sailing and sold his wee boat, which used to be an escape to clear his mind. The wind that brushed through his hair, the waves that lapped and splashed around the boat allowed him to relax in this contrast to his job up in the air. I could only help him by lending an ear and for him to know that I still loved him across the miles that separated us.

With time the fierce ache of longing and hopeless desire became easier to bear, but my love for him stayed rooted deep in my whole being and as these pages come to life with the bitter-sweet memories of our so close to perfect togetherness, tears well up, but at the same time a smile builds, because so many years later we are still in touch and I know it will be so until the day one of us dies.

And when one thought it couldn't – everything just got worse...

Give me Fresh Air – Anywhere

Never quit, never quit…

While sitting in the warmth of my tiny chalet high up in the mountains to where I had retreated when my health condition got really bad, I drifted in and out of memories while the snow was falling in big, soft flakes turning the world outside silently into a winter wonderland. My dogs were napping after our walk.

And once again I wondered how I had survived.

Sipping my hot herbal tea I thought of the three months I was already enjoying the fresh clean air and pure, ice-cold mountain water, which was helping me recuperate. I had started looking for other options, how and where to live the previous autumn, and had often thought how nice it would be to have a small house for myself. It would have to be built organically and allergy friendly, free of the chemicals I had become so sensitive to, following the poisoning, to protect my health. But I didn't have the funds for the land required, nor for the expensive eco-friendly way it would have to be built.

I now couldn't tolerate any smells and fumes from detergents, perfumes or cleaning products anymore, of which the neighbours in the house where I had a flat were using liberally on a daily basis. The fumes were so intense that I could smell them through closed doors and windows. I couldn't sit on my balcony, because the women hung their washing on theirs to dry, and I could smell the detergents in the laundry, which regularly caused nausea and headaches. I couldn't use any of my perfumes anymore. I had become very sensitive indeed.

I did my best not to become paranoid. I tried to live a normal life, and even ignored my body's reactions, trying to force it back to normality and not to react. But, somehow, as I grew older it got worse. Especially since the latest incident which happened on my last birthday. My body's system had no intention of ignoring the toxic environment and reacted in time to even the most minuscule amounts of chemicals.

Together with my friends I had walked into an open-air rooftop restaurant, which had a wooden decking. Two minutes there, we hadn't even ordered yet, I thought the deck was moving. My heart started racing, my neck got stiff, and I could feel my brain. I was sweating and my hands began to shake. Five minutes later I collapsed. Six hours and two saline drips, oxygen and an ER experience with nonplussed doctors later, I was able to get up again. They had examined my allergy passport but were none the wiser. They had no idea why I couldn't move my legs or pronounce words, never mind the dizziness which was relentless and one of my worst episodes ever. They did the usual tests for stroke, heart attack, diabetes and blood pressure, all of which came back with normal readings. The one I managed to suggest they refused to do, saying, although they couldn't know, that that test had nothing to do with my condition. If they would have done it they would have found changed levels indicating an organophosphate poisoning – the test I meant is for AChE (acetyl cholinesterase enzyme)[6] levels and is done, for example, by NATO (ref. Dr Michel Mulder[7]) when soldiers in war zones become unwell. Values below minimum of AChE and BChE[6] are proof of acute intoxication with OP (organophosphorus) nerve gasses[8, 9, 10, 11], and a person should be treated with certain medication (atropine or obidoxime) to help reverse the binding of organophosphorus compounds to the enzyme acetyl cholinesterase.

But they were afraid to do anything or give me any medication after reading the allergy and MCS (multiple chemical sensitivity)[12] pass, so more or less left me to it, and didn't even bother to check with the emergency help centre for poisons, although my friends tried to explain the situation.

Toxic Cocktail

The Dose makes the Poison.

(Said who?)

My friends had figured out what must have been the problem: the wooden decking on the rooftop, still slightly moist from the rain the night before, was now, while drying off in the hot midday sun, emitting steam filled with fumes from flame retardants, fungicides, nano-sized copper-based pesticides and other chemicals, like chromium, all of which the wood was treated with. I got a few lovely nosefuls of that cocktail, its fumes travelling at lightning speed to my brain, upsetting my equilibrium, and rekindling the dreaded symptoms. Two of the three women said that they had smelled a musty, unpleasant mould-like smell, but of course didn't, luckily, have my reactions to them.

It was such a drag, to not know if the next day would be a good day. If I would be able to sleep that night, if I would be able to take my dogs out for their walks, if I would even tolerate my beloved cup of coffee in the morning or the food I would choose to eat during the day. I suddenly wouldn't tolerate cheese, yoghurt, coffee or pasta, or a simple croissant to which I treated myself once in a while.

Often enough, within 20-30 minutes I would have reactions which forced me to lie down. Stiff neck, dizziness, headaches, with or without vomiting, tingling in the hands and feet and weak muscles accompanied such attacks. If it wasn't food, or what was in it, it was some fumes or smells I walked into in supermarkets, or if a building had been renovated or fresh paint was still drying or solvents were being used. It even got to the point that when I happened to walk behind someone on the street who was wearing perfume, and I accidentally caught a 'mouthful', that my throat would swell and my tongue would go all fuzzy. This was usually accompanied by severe headaches for the remainder of the day. I refused to wear a protective mask everywhere and all the time, wanting to force my body and my immune system to 'get over it and get better', but it didn't work. Not always.

If I went off my remedies once in a while, which consisted of a multitude of minerals, enzymes, vitamins and anti-oxidants along with a constant detoxification, I wouldn't last long. Symptoms built up again, the fatigue set in, muscles weakened, the brain fog was back and I had concentration and word-finding problems. In addition, my hearing started to go, but came back after a while.

One day my brother suggested jokingly that living in a mobile home in the wilderness somewhere could be an option and another friend also remarked: "Why not buy a mobile home and drive around the world and stay where you can?" I remembered that when I was a toddler my parents and I lived in a caravan for a while. Dad was searching for a flat and making up his mind which airline he would like to fly for, so we didn't rent a flat, intending to leave soon. I also had lovely memories of New Zealand where we used a mobile home to get around which I had enjoyed immensely and I thought, 'Why not indeed?'

Since fate has this uncanny ability to make these things happen somehow, the very next day another friend sent me an advert with pictures showing a tiny wooden house for sale, with the remark 'in need of some repairs'. It looked like a small wooden, high altitude, sun-blackened chalet with a big terrace and a very pretty interior. It was well furnished with a wood-pellet stove for heating and a small but complete kitchen. The bedroom was large enough for my double bed and it had built-in wardrobes. The plot it stood on was even big enough for a tiny garden and fence for the dogs.

Decisions

The very next day I made an appointment with the seller. I was lucky enough that my symptoms had eased and I could drive, because several days before had been some of those 'very lousy' days following the incident in October, which had landed me in ER. I was having a really hard time after that.

I viewed the tiny house, and liked what I saw. It didn't take long for me to make a decision; everything felt right and there were no offensive smells, and I bought it. It came with everything included at a price I could afford. The beautiful area, a Nature Reservation Park, was in winter a small ski resort and in summer a place for beautiful hikes. I was hooked within the first half hour.

I had become a house owner again, albeit a tiny house, five years after losing my beautiful health farm, which I had built up over fifteen years into which I had invested my whole heart and all the energy I had left. I had to give it up due to my ill health, and because my relationship with someone, who was a very special person, had come to an end. He was very young, much younger than I. It was mainly because he needed to move on, which was not unexpected, and the constant work pressure had created a rift and we had sadly drifted apart; my being unwell did not help, but at the time I wasn't aware of the on-going disastrous changes taking place in my nervous system so I understood, although it was very hard and came at the worst possible moment, but I let him go. It was impossible for me to carry on on my own, although I tried, but soon realised I didn't have the energy, especially after the flight incident when my health really went downhill again, and was worse than in 1997. I found a rent-to-buy tenant who, after a very promising start and the first two instalments never made another payment. She left the place in a totally wrecked state six months after signing the contract. Due to the recession, which had in the meantime hit Europe, I was unable to sell it and had to surrender it lock-stock-and-barrel, in its leftover entirety to the bank. For a long time my heart was broken at the thought of it...

But that was in the past. I now looked at my tiny new home. It really was a miniature mountain chalet. It had no cellar but a large attic, where I could stow my hundreds of books and even have a guest bed or two. Well insulated for the long winters, with many windows allowing lots of sunlight throughout. The additional, unexpected bonus was that the previous owner had never used any paint or wood preservatives, which was just what I needed!

So here I was, remembering years of my life sitting at my table next to the window, and the snow was piling up outside, silently thanking my mother who had passed away half a year earlier, leaving us a little bit of money, just enough for this little abode.

More Memories

Acceptance is the first step to help overcome any consequences of perceived misfortune.

(Bearnairdine Beaumont)

The snow brought me back in my day dreaming to yet another wonderful trip on duty. With three days off in Vancouver I was looking forward to some skiing, intending to head off in the direction of Whistler Mountain. Although I thought I would be on my own, in the end another five crew members joined me. We hopped on the bus early the morning after arrival. Only a few hours later we arrived in Whistler in beautiful sunshine and lots of snow, chattering and laughing in anticipation. We immediately took over a ski hire shop and fitted everyone with skis and everything else we needed. We rented B&B rooms in a beautiful, cosy guesthouse, an Austrian-style chalet, run by a woman originally from there. She cooked breakfast for us while chatting about her life in Whistler Mountain.

What a beautiful environment! We were so lucky; we had the most gorgeous weather, not a cloud to be seen, fabulous snow and lots of it, on which we enjoyed those fantastic wide and long slopes! The super-long 'Peak to Creek' run was amazing, and the area served by the 'Harmony' chairlift was breath taking. The Dave Murray Downhill was a must. It's a black diamond run that's very wide and very fast. I whisked down the slopes enjoying the smooth, huge space and quickly stood in line again for another go. The waiting in line was so much more disciplined than in Europe, where everybody rushes and stands with their skis on your skis, pushing and shoving. But none of that there.

We had such a lot of fun and after an appropriate après-ski evening out would have loved to stay longer. We took the very last possible bus back to the city, just managing to be dropped off at our hotel before minimum rest time would have become hardly any rest time at all, for a few hours' sleep before our return flight that evening.

Then, I was still able to ski – something, that only a short while later became an impossibility, because I lost the power in my legs.

Soon after that flight, I only saw the inside of my hotel rooms; too exhausted to go out with the crew, I ordered room service meals. Too tired and feeling too weak all over to go out as I used to, I just slept as if in a coma most of the time, barely managing the night flights back home.

Wet Dogs and Smelly Socks

I had been on a few Airbus flights on which practically every flight was at one time or another filled with an unbearable stench of kerosene vapours, or the now well-known smelly socks or wet dog smells, or that and a mix of other fumes just before take-off or after landing. The more often it happened, the more I seemed to have a 'doggy's nose' as I called it. My sense of smell, respectively my sensitivity to odours, was increasing. A few flight rotations later I was so extremely tired that I dropped off to sleep at the dinner table in the middle of eating a plate of soup. And not only once, this started happening regularly. I was not able to recuperate at night. I was not sleeping well, going to bed and waking up with headaches and a general feeling of 'I can feel my brain'. Brain fog with all its symptoms of confusion, forgetfulness, lack of focus and clarity was bothering me all the time, and I did nothing much else but sleep a heavy sleep during the rest times at home. I constantly had sore muscles as if I had done some crazy exercising, but hadn't, or as if I had a bad flu. I felt off balance, clumsy and kept tripping over myself, missing steps. One morning after a flight I woke with my right eye so swollen I couldn't open it, red, blotchy and itchy skin covered my whole face once again and, in addition, not only my lower arms up to the elbows were itchy and the skin was bone dry and red, but the back of my neck and shoulders as well.

I went to the physician, who, until years later, was the only one who always listened, and always did his best to help me. At first he couldn't figure out what was wrong. Hearing about all my other symptoms and after some tests, during which he also came up with tachycardia, he first put it all down to contact dermatitis or a dermal allergic reaction, and later diagnosed multiple chemical sensitivity (MCS)[12]. Which is much more than others have ever acknowledged, and many even deny such a thing exists. He decided to order the laboratory to test for pesticides. When the results came back they showed levels of permethrin (pyrethroid)[4, 8, 9, 10, 11], DDT, lindane and formaldehyde in my blood. Looking angry, the doctor exclaimed with some irritation: "Where the hell did all that come from?"

Other chemicals weren't analysed because, like me, they didn't know what they were looking for or that they should have looked for more. We knew that the permethrin was used in the aerosol sprays, as was indicated on the cans, and had to assume that in manufacturing, ingredients such as DDT and formaldehyde were used but possibly not declared, as well as solvents, and perhaps propellants.

This was also the first time he discovered that my reflexes were impaired. He mentioned peripheral neuropathy, which is a term that describes damage to one or more peripheral nerves, due to the numbness in my hands and feet. The damage means that the messages that travel within the central nervous system are disrupted. All other reasons bar toxicity were ruled out. Poisons such as pesticides or solvents can cause this disruption. He was disgusted.

So far so good. I seemed to have a name for my problems and where I had acquired them. But what to do? A month or so later I came across an article in our flight attendants' union's newsletter. At that time the union leaders were supportive and not yet afraid to put facts on the table and be our voice. They were not yet cautious of unpleasant dealings with the company management, who not yet had a hold over them. The article spoke about dangers to our health from on-board spraying and that the ingredients could be the reason for ill health. They had listed all of my symptoms.

I called them and finally found more help.

Nights in Bangkok

If everything is gotten dreamily,
it will go away dreamily too.

(Buddhist proverb)

In the meantime I was on duty as usual and dispatched on several flights, one of which was to Thailand in February 1996. Five days off and so much to see! Although I was shattered after the long flight, which was my usual condition these days, I pulled myself together and took off on a tour with one of the girls and one of the pilots and his wife. A very early start made viewing the amazing palace a pleasure, as it was very quiet with only a few tourists and the sun not too hot early in the day.

Ever since I had read about the incredible journey of the great Emerald Buddha, I wanted to see it in its home in Bangkok. The story went that the Emerald Buddha statue was discovered when lightning struck a pagoda in a temple in Chiang Rai, after which something became visible beneath the stucco. I walked into the temple. Many worshippers were kneeling and praying at the base of a huge mountain of Buddhist relics, statues and pictures surrounded by flowers and candles and burning incense. The Emerald Buddha sat on top of the relics, like a star or angel on a Christmas tree. I sat for a while amongst the devotees and just let the atmosphere soak in. When I exited the temple, I walked into a sea of tourists who had just arrived. After the peace and quiet in the temple the hubbub of hundreds of people chattering in multiple languages was an assault to my senses.

Squeezing through the crowd milling around me, I managed to get close to another temple from where I could hear chanting which had attracted me. I sat at the base of a huge old tree close by and listened for a while. One wasn't allowed in that temple so as not to disturb the monks in their prayers.

We returned to the hotel by boat, along Chao Phraya River, which is a different way to explore parts of Bangkok. Cruising down the river we had wonderful views of Bangkok's riverside areas with its many historical attractions, and we also got to explore the 'klongs' for a glimpse of yesteryear Bangkok.

Of course we also visited the famous night markets and shopped until we dropped, including additional bags and suitcases to take everything home, and went for delicious Thai food dinners. I just had to get the various spices at a local spice and vegetable market, in which not many tourists could be found, making the experience very special. We went to Pahurat also known as the Little India of Bangkok. Pahurat, just as lively, loud and colourful as in India itself with the Indian community selling an unbelievably huge selection of beautiful textiles and colourful sarees, jewellery, footwear and of course, spices. The air was loaded with the scents of all the spices and incense, which transported me right back to Bombay. Those spicy fragrances were a delight to my senses and didn't bother me in the least.

In retrospect I would be glad that I went on that sightseeing tour, because...

Contaminated

...a few months later I left on an Airbus four-day flight rotation, covering three to four legs a day to various European destinations, never suspecting it was to be my last!

I had been feeling very poorly for a very long time now, in fact I got worse since re-training on to Airbuses. I had to take sick leave more often than not, struggled to go to work, and felt worse with dizzy spells and constant headaches on practically every flight. I couldn't stand those smells of dirty wet socks (or was it wet dogs?), which seemed to be present on every aircraft and always more intense than the previous time, which we still thought was normal after a long night flight and full house; the fumes of kerosene before take-off, and exhaust fumes that wafted through the cabin while on blocks or taxiing made me feel nauseous instantly. I continued having trouble with my balance and started having problems when the pilots changed heading, and when the aircraft moved to change direction or if descent was too fast. The movement made me feel dizzy; it felt like my brain was detached from my body, and my skull felt too tight with that pressure building up that felt like my brain was swollen and inflamed, putting pressure on my hearing. Often it took a day or two for that to settle down again. Now my doctors thought I was having low blood pressure problems...

Over the past months a new symptom had appeared. I was now in constant pain. Excruciating sciatic nerve pain had joined the muscular flu-like ache. Often I could barely sit or stand, never mind walk, without being bent over double. I had been receiving up to thirty injections of pain and muscle relaxant medicines which were administered along my spine twice a week to help that, but it always only lasted a couple of hours. The muscles were rock hard, the sciatic nerve area remained so painful, I could hardly move. Puzzled because other typical symptoms such as damaged or slipped discs weren't apparent, the orthopaedic surgeon's only other solution was exploratory surgery to 'perhaps find something that way', which I refused.

Who would have thought that toxins could also affect the spinal cord, which is the central trunk of nerves connecting the brain with the rest of the body?

Nerves and nerve roots become irritated and radiate pain from chemicals! The central nervous system (CNS), which is in the spinal trunk, was already irritated and damage was done, and the muscles were filled with toxins. So the sciatic nerve wasn't jammed at all, it was radiating pain from the toxins! Again, another symptom of peripheral neuropathy[13, 14, 15] due to toxic stress.

And as for the muscles, the toxins concentrate in parts of the muscle and that irritates them to contract; they stiffen and feel like rocks, immovable and pulling in all the wrong directions. I couldn't walk, sit or lie without pain. And again, no matter what I said, they dismissed the thought of a chronic poisoning being the possible reason.

Flying frequently can be hazardous to your health.

<u>This is especially true for those who do it for a living.</u>

My whole system finally broke down.

Two days into the rotation I had to ask for a stand-by to fill in for me and I deadheaded back home by train. But only after lying for over two hours in the airport's emergency room waiting for the dizziness and pressure in the brain to pass.

I made it back to base and was driving home when I had to stop the car because I felt so dizzy and so very fatigued that my eyes kept closing. Somehow I just fell asleep right after stopping the car at the side of the road. I woke a couple of hours later; my hands and legs were tingling and felt numb. Hardly able to concentrate, and trying to figure out through the brain fog what I was doing at the side of the road, I then had to figure out how to handle the car. I sat for a while staring at the wheel, then remembered that I had to start the engine by turning the key; but then I couldn't get the car to move, until I realised that I was stepping on the brakes instead of the accelerator. I cried. I was so tired and frustrated at this. Concentrating hard I managed to get home.

I went straight to bed and woke up eighteen hours later looking like someone had bashed me in the face, my right eye swollen shut again, head throbbing, feeling like it was packed tight and overfull with wet cotton wool, no brain, and pressure on my ears, not feeling rested at all. The terrible pain in my head seemed to travel right down my spine and was killing me, and I couldn't see straight; it felt like I had a steel band around my head just above my eyes and around the base of my skull. My neck was in a strange way stiff and painful, and my pillow was covered in lots more of the already thinning hair[16]. The feeling of extreme weakness and aching muscles barely let me get up from my bed. I felt very unsteady and, stumbling, had to concentrate hard to set one foot in front of the other.

If not before, I now definitely knew that something was very wrong and something had to be done. Now.

I would much rather continue with fun stories of flights to beautiful, interesting and colourful places, but the reason for the deterioration of my once excellent health is the most important part and the main subject of why I am sharing my life's story. The information contained in what is to follow is meant to help professional aviators, frequent flyers, and passengers on a holiday trip alike, to become informed aviation industry customers. The possible toxic cocktail in your blood which you may well have acquired on your flights could be causing those problems you have been having lately. Professional athletes, who fly a lot, may have to consider in future when they are tested for substances, to also test for this kind of substance, since they could be mimicking other, but 'illegal', substances. The toxins can disrupt our whole system and make us weak, extremely tired, and unable to function, as they aggressively attack the central nervous system and can cause, over time, serious damage. Legally.

Anyone frequently flying, which means once or more a week, is repeatedly exposed and is especially at risk.

My Odyssey Began

Knowledge is Power, Wisdom is Strength,
and Learning is Courage.

Doctors followed others; practically each one giving me different information, diagnoses or the brilliant suggestion to go for therapy, because 'it's all in your head'.

Yes, it was in my head, to be more specific in the brain, but not in the way they meant. I knew that seeing a shrink was firstly not necessary, because psychologically and emotionally I felt fine, and never had been inclined to phobias or hypochondria. Secondly, once in the system of psychology and psychiatry, it was more than difficult to get out of it again. One was more or less marked, as if one was wearing a stamp on one's forehead, and after categorical diagnoses of mental imbalance, each and every symptom would be put down to emotional problems!

"Psychiatry has the advantage, unique in the medical field, that it can invent illnesses, and relax the criteria for these illnesses, more or less at will. Psychiatry, unlike other medical specialities, has no natural limits to its growth potential. They can continue to expand the diagnostic net until everybody in the world has a diagnosis. But it doesn't even have to stop there. They can go for everybody having two, three, four, etc., diagnoses. If organised psychiatry votes an illness into being, there is no reality that can act as a brake or a check on this activity." (Philip Hickey PhD)[17]

I researched in the medical press, dug around in libraries, read medical books, searched in the natural medicine field and newspapers, and that was the time our union released an article about the dangers of the aerosol sprays and the ingredients used, specifically the very toxic pesticide called permethrin. I called them and was given the number of an elderly professor who finally put a name and a cause to my problem. He added me to the study he was conducting and did his tests, after which he said: "You are severely poisoned, my dear!"

Poisoned by the neurotoxic agent permethrin belonging to a range of chemicals called 'organophosphates' (pyrethroids) which were used as an ingredient in the aerosol sprays for disinsection. And as I would learn in the future, I was also poisoned from constant exposure to jet engine oil fumes polluting the cabin through bleed air, which also contains various neurotoxic agents of a similar kind, and not to forget the kerosene vapours.

So, I was diagnosed with chronic permethrin poisoning, respiratory distress and allergic asthma, which had been confirmed by the blood tests I mentioned earlier. And that is what the airline's flight medic wrote on my final visit, discharging me on medical grounds. All other symptoms were ignored.

I never set foot in uniform on an aircraft again.

I had taken a can of aerosol spray home with me, to get it analysed and hopefully discover the undeclared 'trade secret' ingredients, like e.g. DDT. I gave it to the union leadership who promised me it would be sent to an independent laboratory. I never received results. The can had vanished into thin air and was never tested.

It didn't take long for TV stations and newspaper journalists to contact me, wanting an interview, sent in my direction by the union. Due to my newly acquired knowledge, my anger, my newly awakened rebellious nature and thus willingness to talk with them, I was interesting. Nobody else came forward although there were many more colleagues with health issues. Some wrote me notes, most of them anonymous, thanking me for stepping up and for being rebellious and unafraid, but no one offered active support.

So I was alone out there and, for a while, the subject of flight attendants being poisoned on the job went through the German media. An interesting thing happened though. The more vocal I became, the less the people in our union, who previously gladly helped me, were available to me. And one day, I received a warning from one of them that I should be careful and rather not be too outspoken, that trouble was in the air. No more interviews took place, and previously promised legal support through the union was denied with very superficial reasons.

A little later I went for a check-up to my obstetrician and got another fright when he said there was a tumour, which he thought to be the beginning stages of cervical cancer. He was very good, and got me to one of the best hospitals the very next day and performed immediate surgery. His diagnosis was confirmed – I was very lucky that it was caught early.

This too, as I knew later, was most likely a cellular reaction to chronic (long-term) low level (LTLL) exposure[18] and to sometimes acute, high levels of toxicity when a fume event took place I had been exposed to. Poisoning.

I was aghast, angry and disappointed, all at the same time, that I should have to go through so much ill health caused by something I was ordered to do by my employer! How could they do that? They knew that the stuff was dangerous, I was sure of that. Why didn't the aviation medics do anything about it? It turned out that thousands of crew were affected, but their files were hidden away in a back room, which a friend of mine found out years later, when one of the flight crew physicians in some sudden mood swing showed her, and actually said: "Tell me, what can we do?" and "Remember who my boss is."

What can we do? How about stepping up and speaking up about what was going on? And where were all the voices from the affected colleagues? Did they actually know why they were sick, and what caused it? This information was of course presumably classified.

I followed the advice I was given by the union and filed for the workers' compensation claim, for which it was mandatory to pay big sums of money every month, which was deducted automatically from the wages. Of course making us think we were well prepared and covered for all eventualities.

I was put through 'expert' testing by this insurance, of course by experts of their choice: an internist who also boasted allergology as an additional speciality, an orthopaedic surgeon, and of course a psychiatrist. No toxicologist or neurologist.

They put me through 'rigorous' examinations, which consisted for instance in me having to bend over, touch my fingers to the floor and after prodding along my back muscles, and making me turn my head to the right and left, the orthopaedic surgeon found nothing wrong with me. The psychiatrist diagnosed that in his opinion I was having a hard time after my divorce (this examination was five years later!). He also found that I was a bit difficult to handle since I refused to undergo a so-called provocation test, during which the patient is seated in a tiny cubicle and is exposed to a substance or 'thing' that is claimed to provoke a response to see if one really reacted to them. The internist/allergologist, whom I had asked if his intention was to kill me, would have done this. It seems they didn't approve of me expressing my worries.

So obviously they were exchanging notes, which of course would lead to bias. All of them wrote 'expert testimonies' summing up that they could find nothing wrong with me, except that I was a 'difficult' patient and everything or anything they observed came down to stress. I wonder how they could sleep at night.

Four years, three lawyers, several judges, and mountains of files later, my application was denied.

From the beginning they had denied that 'permethrin poisoning' was in any way workplace related or even a recognised job hazard, in which case, they stated, it would have been listed on their ICD list of recognised illnesses (International Classification of Diseases ICD-10), which it was not and therefore non-existent. Nothing my own highly qualified experts wrote in their expertise applied according to them, and everything was categorically swiped off the table. It had been a four-year battle, and I did not have the funds to carry on. This particular work compensation insurance company is very close and, so I have been told, even partially owned by the airline I worked for.

In 2012, after a lot of studying to increase my knowledge, I pulled out that old file, and noticed that on the very first page of the case denial text, they had dismissed it, quoting the wrong toxin, along with the wrong ICD-10 number and argued wrong medical facts; but it was too late. Someone, a lawyer as a matter of fact who gave a speech at some conference I attended later that same year, said one could re-open such cases even after many years had elapsed; there was no timeframe to them. I immediately called several lawyers. But each lawyer, after hearing what it was about and who the defendant was to be, was suddenly very busy and not available!

Was it surprising that my then lawyer missed the wrong referencing and ICD-10 numbers in the documents? Or did he?

Dr Raymond Singer, who is a knowledgeable forensic expert says: "Neurotoxicity, poisoning of the brain and nervous system, is a well-documented effect of exposure to many widely used chemicals, yet doctors, and lawyers often fail to recognise it."

So I received no ill-health pension and no workplace-related ill-health or accident compensation. Not from the German insurance. I did get a recognition (without legal actions necessary) from the Swiss organisation, who approved a 52% invalidity and paid me monthly a €100 disability support which doesn't even cover my remedies. So why the difference?

My new life began to evolve around my little health farm and I tried to forget what had brought me there.

The Day Everything Came Flooding Back

I was busy keeping up to date with health-related information, digging around on the Internet for information on pesticides in general, when I one day came across this, via the key word 'permethrin':

"In 2010 WHO published that what we had been worried about for years now – they said that an insecticide of high acute toxicity, meeting the criteria of class Ia or Ib of the WHO Recommended Classification of Pesticides by Hazard (WHO, 2010), is not recommended for use in aircraft disinsection."[19]

A bit late for many others and me!

Then, in 2012, I was diagnosed with 'severe central nervous system damage due to organophosphate poisoning'.

And all the symptoms and worse came back after taking this ONE flight as a regular passenger. What had happened?

I had received an invitation from a former colleague, who was a victim of contaminated cabin air herself, to give a speech at a health conference in which the subject of aircraft aerosol spraying was listed in the programme. I bought a ticket for the flight with my old employer airline thinking I was safe, since there would be no aerosol spraying on this short-range flight. That thought alone showed that I was still not 100 percent educated in contamination of cabin air and chemical reactions.

The flight was late in departure, with us sitting on board for about forty minutes before we finally took off. Arriving in the Frankfurt air space, the captain announced a holding pattern due to much traffic. When we finally landed and were taxiing to our parking position, another announcement from the cockpit let us know that we had to stop and were told to wait on the 'apron', an area where aircraft are parked and serviced, because our designated parking position was still occupied by another aircraft.

And that's when it happened!

A few minutes into waiting, during which I was wondering why the pilots were revving the engines in neutral, the cabin suddenly filled with very bad smelling fumes, like foul eggs and vomit which, within seconds, and although I immediately covered my face with my scarf, which of course was way too skimpy to protect me, made me feel nauseous. My heart started racing, my brain went all 'mushy', then I felt slightly dizzy, and seconds later I felt a headache coming on and my neck stiffening. The passenger beside me commented on the stench and also covered his nose. I got off the aircraft as fast as I could when the doors were finally opened, hoping to get some fresh air.

As it turned out this aircraft's cabin air (Airbus A320) and that of the return flight's was contaminated with jet-engine oil fumes! I had previously not known about these fumes and how dangerous they could be, but at that health conference my eyes were finally opened.

After arrival I was already barely able to function. The headache was relentless and I felt like I had just come off a ship, walking with unsteady sea legs, but I forced myself through it and it eased after an hour or two. Later on, listening to other speakers, I was introduced to highly toxic ingredients in jet engine oils; leaking seals, bleed air and neurotoxic injury caused by contaminated cabin air from specific chemicals in the oil. They dubbed it Aerotoxic Syndrome.

I was stunned to say the least.

It's Classified

Nobody had ever mentioned this while I was still flying, nor when I was getting all those tests done. But I learned that it was a known fact since as early as the mid-1950s. Exposure to heated jet engine oils was found to be highly toxic by military sources in 1954. Studies were conducted and internally published as far back as 1944. Of course, highly classified information, which was inconvenient for the aviation and connected industry, these studies were not made public. And it was the time of the Cold War. As military aircraft were affected, that formed the 'backbone' of the strategic force, it may be understood why this issue was treated so secretly.

In 1955 one Henry A Redall stated that air bled from the compressors of turbojet engines is contaminated because of internal oil leaks and wrote a study on the subject. He also described several methods of elimination to avoid the problem, saying that: "Air bled from the compressors of some high compression ratio turbojet engines is contaminated because of internal engine oil leakage into the compressor air. External leakage of oil or other fluids wherein such fluids can leak into the engine air inlet can also cause contamination. There are two positive methods of elimination..."[20]

Nothing has been done.

Back to my case: I was given a special air sampler for the return flight from the health conference which I had turned on from doors closed to just before doors opened in Dublin. It was then analysed in a well-known independent laboratory in Germany; and the results came back with way too high levels of TCP (tricresyl-phosphate)[21, 22, 23] and other contaminants which only could come from jet engine oil, since it showed the specific 'fingerprint' of these oils. Of course, later they tried to discredit the air sampler and the results, even insinuating that I hadn't used it professionally.

So, I had an injury caused by something invisible; by air I breathed twenty days and nights of practically every month over twenty years, which not only I trusted to be as *pure as the air in an operating theatre*; instead it had caused severe neurological damage in the central nervous system[24] through chronic exposure to neurotoxic chemicals[25, 26, 27]. This was not new knowledge but it seems classified.

Unbelievable isn't it?

To put it into a few words: this meant that my brain was damaged from toxins I had inhaled on board. First at my work place, then I got a 'refill' as a passenger.

My employers and the aviation industry altogether had allowed the use of neurotoxic chemicals and although they knew of the dangers since the 1950s had done nothing to change it. What an incredible shock. I felt as if I was in some sort of science fiction horror movie.

The Verdict

Justice will not be served until those who are unaffected are as outraged as those who are.

(Benjamin Franklin)

A specific blood test[24, 28], which was developed by Professor Abou-Donia, determined and confirmed 'severe OP (organophosphate) induced neurological damage', a specific type of brain cell injury which can only happen through contact with organophosphates.

I was appalled that it was so bad; the numbers, swimming in front of my eyes were so high bar one, and were marked with three stars ranking them in the top levels of injury in comparison to the normal control levels listed. However, at the same time I knew it had to be the case since I had been having some of the most awful symptoms. As you can imagine, I was very worried about the fact of having brain damage!

I was told it was 'probably irreversible'. Most of it.

It turned out that the MCS[12] I was diagnosed with was, as in many other cases, an illness following an organophosphate poisoning, as Professor Martin Pall describes it, Multiple Chemical Sensitivity (MCS), also known as chemical sensitivity and Toxicant-Induced Loss of tolerance (TILT), which is a disease that is initiated by toxic chemical exposure leading to brain injury. It produces a high level of sensitivity to the same set of chemicals that were the initiation of the disease.[29]

MCS follows usually within about two years. The neurological symptoms can also appear as late as that. This is called a delayed reaction: OPIDN (Organophosphate Induced Delayed Neuropathy). It is a neuropathy caused by the killing of neurons in the central nervous system, especially in the spinal cord, as a result of acute or chronic organophosphate poisoning.

Many studies clearly show that the MCS mechanism sets in either after short-term exposure to high concentrations of chemicals, or long-term exposure to low dose amounts of chemicals (LTLL).[17] From first exposure to the beginning of actual symptoms years can go by. During this time a self-dynamic biochemical mechanism develops within the cells of the central nervous system (CNS), the immune system and the endocrine system, which leads to a generalised and systematic picture of ill health, in which inflammatory processes are activated that have a direct influence on the stress hormone system and the functions of the CNS. (Research on Multiple Chemical Sensitivity (MCS) – Compiled by Professor Anne C. Steinemann and Amy L. Davis, University of Washington.)

In my case, the 'chronic' low-level exposure, including several strong smell and at least one fume event I remember, was definitively fact; another fact was the additional exposure to pesticides on so many routes, when we had to spray the aircraft overhead of the unsuspecting passengers. Of course the additional residue build-up from previous spraying on any of the aircraft must not be forgotten. One should know that the whole aircraft were fully disinsected (residual spraying), including galleys, toilets, hold, everything, on a regular basis for hygiene reasons, which resulted in the upholding and presence of constant levels of contamination, with even stronger, more potent mixes of pesticides.

The Material Safety Data Sheet by another major oil company states that it: "May contain mixed isomers of tricresyl phosphate. Tricresyl phosphate may be absorbed either through the skin, by ingestion or by inhalation. *These effects are delayed and may be permanent depending upon the degree of exposure.* However, the concentration of these harmful isomers of TCP in this product is so low that neurotoxic effects are not expected."[30]

Just to let it sink in: brain damage, respiratory problems and MCS as a result from bleed air, leaking seals, the ingredients in jet engine oils and fumes therefrom, and indoor pesticide use!

Double Poisoning

When I was diagnosed with the permethrin poisoning in 1996 I followed the advice I was given by Prof Müller-Mohnsson. He was an expert in the field of pesticide poisonings, who, unafraid and very outspoken, fought for the cause of people poisoned by organophosphates up to the very day he died in 2010. He advised: "No contact with chemicals of any kind, avoid them like the plague, no stress, fresh air, fresh water, organic food, detoxification programme, and a special combination of high dose vitamins, minerals and enzymes – and do not ever fly again!"

The list of do not dos was long, but since I was only 43 and wanted to regain my health I followed his advice to the T. It took me about two years to feel big improvements. Some symptoms stayed with me, which I had been warned about by the professor, but I was able to live with them. The extreme fatigue eased off, my hair grew back, the dizziness went, allergies improved and some even disappeared; the muscle weakness, although less severe, and frequent headaches stayed, as did the sciatic pain for another few years.

I had to work, because I had to after not receiving any compensation or pension. So I was not able to just concentrate on my health, but I made a plan and managed well enough. I built up my little health farm together with my then partner in the middle of nowhere in the heart of Ireland, financing it with a small life insurance I had luckily set up following Dad's advice, which was paid out when I stopped flying. We managed and were successfully offering complementary health treatments, nutritional advice, and later on also accredited courses in complementary health modalities. We even registered and trademarked our own back and spine treatment, which my partner had developed over the years. We offered B&B, which slowly turned into a busy, small guesthouse with people staying for weekends or even weeks sometimes. Following my lifelong interest in naturopathy I studied and qualified in several naturopathic modalities, and kept myself up to date at all times.

Up until that fatal day when I chose to fly instead of drive by car to Germany, all went well. I hardly had any very bad symptoms any more, except if I inadvertently managed to be exposed to chemicals, which I took care not to let happen.

The sensitivity remained, but I thought I would be fine.

Melt Down

Back home from the health conference, I became very sick. The headaches got worse and were relentless day-in day-out. The extreme fatigue and muscle weakness were back, my neck stiff and this time the stiffness travelled right down my spine. I was forced to cancel my clients day, after day, after day.

Then came that horrible night about three weeks later. I woke with a start, my heart pounding. I tried to focus, then realised I couldn't, because first I thought it was an earthquake, then I thought I was having a stroke when I became aware of the extreme pain in my head. It was excruciating; when I moved, it felt like I was in a major storm on a ship, the whole house was moving. A most horrific dizziness with sensations of rolling up, down and sideways. I felt terrible and tried hard to focus. I noticed numbness and tingling in my hands and legs; when I tried to move I realised I actually had no feeling in my legs. My spine seemed to hang in mid-air somehow, and I could feel sensations like electrical charges within it. Everything seemed detached and I shut my eyes, hoping to stop the dizziness. For a terrifying moment I thought blurry thoughts like: 'This is it, your final hour has arrived' and 'Help somebody, please', while trying to force my breathing to calm down.

At some point I managed to more or less fall out of bed and drag myself on my elbows ever so slowly, feeling terribly sick, to the kitchen, where I tried to get hold of the phone to call for help. But I couldn't focus on the numbers, the dial was moving all over the place, the floor was moving, the walls were moving, the whole house was heaving – so I just sat in a rigid motionlessness under the table, eyes closed tight trying to stabilise myself by placing my numb hands on the floor; waiting, waiting for the pain and the horrific dizziness to pass. My dogs lay close by, watching me, sensing something was very wrong... until the motions eased a bit and I was able to focus and dial the number to call my brother, hours later.

Several days later the symptoms became less, every few hours a repetition of the dizzy spell happened but not as bad or as long. Unable to do anything else, I just lay on my bed, as still as a mummy, waiting for my brain to stand still, afraid to move to not activate it, and sleeping fitfully with three or four pillows under my head because I couldn't lie flat. I couldn't eat; I just drank some water knowing that my body needed it to function. I was not about to give in to this whatever it was. I concentrated, I focussed, I breathed, I talked to myself and my body, I did everything I kept telling my patients to do to feel better. One day, although it had eased, I couldn't stand the recurring dizziness anymore and called my brother's physician. I had avoided this because I had lost all faith in the medical profession over the years and doubted that there would be anyone in this country who knew about MCS or organophosphate poisoning. With much difficulty, because I couldn't find the words, I explained my predicament. He was understanding, but admitted that he had no toxicological background and prescribed a medication so I could cope with the dizziness, but the tablets came right back up again – my body was incapable of dealing with more chemicals. After constantly taking them anyway, at some stage they stayed down and helped a bit.

Slowly, slowly, about three weeks later, I felt at least half normal again. Terribly weak, I couldn't take two steps up the stairs without having to pause, but alive.

These episodes stayed with me ever since, some as bad, some less, plus some new symptoms. One time I went to bed fine, but when I tried to get up in the morning, I couldn't. I couldn't move, because if I did my body screamed in pain – every inch of me was pain, pain, pain. I realised that I couldn't hear either. What a horrific experience!

Once again I dragged myself to the kitchen, supporting myself on furniture, groping along the walls, and then I watched myself as in a surreal dream, trying to lift a glass with some water in it. I lifted it with both hands, while leaning against the kitchen cabinet for support. I realised with amazement that I had no strength whatsoever left and the pain in my hands prevented me to hold and lift the 'heavy' glass – what was happening to me? Why couldn't I even lift a glass of water?

Once again I lay motionless, waiting, sleeping, waiting, until the pain started to ease off, and four days later I started feeling better. My hearing came back along with the brain pain leaving. I had to use a cane to get around after that to stabilise myself.

Each episode has been in connection with an exposure to chemicals. Some vapours I may have inadvertently walked in to; it only took a few breaths, but inhaling a load of toxic fumes and sometimes without realising that they were present, since they can be free from pungent odours, was enough. The fumes with their 'nano' load of various chemicals travel with lightning speed through the CNS straight to the brain and unleash the dreaded, horrible reactions. The initial poisoning from the contaminated cabin air over so many years had sensitised my system so much that exposure to any chemicals became a hazard I had to reckon with at any given time, and suffer the consequences.

After receiving the shocking results from the air sampler and the even worse blood test results, plus several expert diagnoses, the dormant warrior in me awoke again and I gathered my remaining energy and filed a personal injury lawsuit, based on the Montreal Convention for Passenger Rights against the airline – more about that later on.

The Questions One Asks

Justice?

Wondering why on Earth this happened to me twice I decided that there had to be a reason; whatever it might be I felt that I needed to become involved in making this known, as I had done previously. The sense of injustice and the anger at an industry blatantly playing with the health of their employees and their clients was unacceptable. Their ease at sowing doubt by claiming knowledge they don't have to wrangle themselves out of liability was, and is, amazing, and how certain experts fall for it, even more. Instead of forcing them to prove it, the sick person is forced to do so. How, when they claim 'trade secret' rights and use doubtful 'legal limits' as last resorts to enforce their claims of innocence? There was no excuse good enough they could invent, nor their arrogant, know-it-all comments claiming 'too low levels to be harmful' would do, not even if it were 'only' one person who was injured! They have no right to use toxic material that can cause severe ill health and even deaths. It is human lives they are gambling with! None of them would rise to the challenge and expose themselves to a fume event, which could easily be reproduced. Why not if they say it's harmless?

This time I wouldn't be on my own though. Together with my new friends I had been introduced to at the health conference, I learned a lot about the subject and illness they called Aerotoxic Syndrome, and that so many were affected, especially flight crew and many frequent flyers. I got to work with the people who were tirelessly gathering evidence, publishing material and campaigning to create awareness in the public and aviation industry. More and more aviators and also passengers called for help and information. More and more crew members and passengers suddenly had a name for their ill health, after finally finding those who listened and who were able to tell them what was going on and send them to those physicians who knew the cause and how to help.

I wanted to share my experience and also the know-how to get better. I wanted to make sure that everybody knew about this atrocity and that even the doubters realised that they, too, could be next in line to be harmed by contaminated cabin air.

To all professional aviators, all you frequent flyers, managers, CEOs, journalists and professional athletes who fly nearly as much as the crews do; mothers and fathers, listen, read, be informed. You never know: the nauseous feeling, the vomiting, headache and dizziness, the fatigue and flu-like symptoms that won't go away that you may be experiencing after a flight or even during the flight, could have to do with an invisible predator: a toxic cocktail lingering in the air you are breathing while harming your central nervous system! The only things that are trying to filter this cocktail of toxic substances, but without succeeding, are your lungs. And without a doubt it is much worse than cigarette smoke.

Toxic cocktail?

Yes. There's not only the bleed air and disinsectant spraying, there's also flame retardants in carpets and other materials, plastic interiors, plasticisers, solvents, lubricants and kerosene fumes, of which you will read about further on.

Back to the Present

I have put together a simple introduction to the why and how one can become so sick from contaminated cabin air, and hope that I have made it transparent and easy to read. For more in-depth information and for technical details, please refer to one of the websites or to the thirty odd videos and documentaries on YouTube to which you can link via the aerotoxic.org or aerotoxicteam.com websites or directly on YouTube. Just punch in 'Aerotoxic Syndrome'.

I am sharing the knowledge I have gathered over the years in the attempt to help you, who may also be a victim of contaminated cabin air. Years of research and working with other victims, cabin crew and pilots, friends, colleagues, scientists and physicians, and the collection of their experience have amounted to a massive amount of evidence.

With the know-how, and by using myself as a 'guinea pig' for so many years to determine what really helps to improve the condition and what doesn't, I think I can give you a fairly comprehensive overview from which you have a starting point to help yourself. Or use it as a help to work with your health practitioner or physician, for whom the subject will be more likely than not a novelty. So please learn to be an informed patient.

Try not to go to umpteen physicians – if you are at a loss, rather contact us at Aerotoxic Association or Aerotoxic Team on the helpline to get the list of recommended physicians which we all have been in touch with one way or another.

Also, any other information based on facts, and which are not classified anymore, can be found on our dedicated websites or by contacting us.

Part 2

Toxic Cocktail ‘par excellence’

Toxic Cocktail

Prevention is better than cure.

(Desiderius Erasmus)

No it's not as pristine as the air in an operating theatre – which is what they told us in our training.

When you think about airplane cabin air, it's likely you first think about catching a virus or other germs that get passed through the plane's circulation system. But this is the least of your worries.

'Aerotoxic Syndrome' is the 'official' name coined by Professor Chris Winder († 2014) from Australia, Dr Harry Hofmann, USA († 2004) and Dr Jean Christophe Balouet from France back in 1999. It is used to identify the long list of both acute and chronic symptoms crew members and passengers have suffered, caused by inhaling contaminated aircraft cabin air. Symptoms include dizziness, headaches, chronic fatigue, respiratory difficulties, vision problems, brain fog, tremors and other neurological symptoms during, and after, their flight.

Governments and the WHO (World Health Organisation) like to talk about lower or upper limits that, according to them, are within the range of tolerability, usually stating that certain values tested are sub-marginal and, as such, present no danger to human health. Ever. Without taking into account that the entire world population cannot really be identical in how each person reacts or doesn't to pollution and individual chemicals or mixtures thereof.

Even after inhaling small quantities, or so-called 'low level' amounts of contaminant particles, pilots and flight attendants like myself have suffered long-term neurological symptoms that are the result of *long-term low level* exposure to aircraft engine oil contaminants and other toxic chemicals polluting the on-board breathing air, e.g. the infamous aerosol pesticide spraying and kerosene vapours. Never mind the possible fume event, which covers everybody on board in toxic smoke!

The term 'Aerotoxic Syndrome' has been widely used since it came to life, but I prefer the term 'Aerotoxic Injury', since injury to the brain or parts of the brain and nervous system is what the toxic soup causes. Experts (on the other side of the fence) blatantly deny any connection between the multitude of symptoms and the toxins, and ridicule the word 'syndrome'. They tend to say that it is neither a validated nor proven illness and that the literature that describes it has not been peer-reviewed. Pardon me, but the literature was (peer)-reviewed before publication, was it not? Other industry experts even say it is some form of psychological disorder; one even stated it is all due to 'hyperventilation', which would mean that (due to the way it was described) all pilots hyperventilate during the flight and especially during the landing phase, and due to that 'sometimes' have to don their oxygen masks. I am sure all pilots love to be told they are so nervous of the landing phase and therefore hyperventilate so badly that they have to have oxygen to be able to function.

Many listed illnesses end with the word syndrome attached to a name of the scientist who discovered it (Tourette's Syndrome, Parkinson's Syndrome, Cushing's Syndrome, etc.). There is also more to say regarding the diagnosis of 'psychological issues'. Psychological disorders cannot be proven and psychologists and psychiatrists have a wide range of possibilities to fabricate an illness.

Symptoms of Aerotoxic Syndrome may be reversible for some people, which can even happen fairly quickly. However, lasting neurological damage as a result of even low-level but long-term exposure is common. We have even had some people become severely ill from one exposure to a fume event. Many, if not all, will experience MCS (Multiple Chemical Sensitivity) in the wake of a (long-term, chronic, low-level) poisoning, which usually sets in 1-2 years after the initial symptoms have appeared. In my case I gradually got worse, and am now dealing with full-blown MCS, never mind the remaining neurological episodes.

When one is chemical sensitive, it means that low molecular weight chemicals bind to chemoreceptors on sensory nerve fibres, which leads to the release of inflammatory mediators. A long-term exposure can lead to an adaptation phenomenon, meaning that the body sees the situation as the norm and will now react to a multitude of other irritants[27, 31].

The Air You and I Breathe

Planes were designed with mechanical compressors that produced clean, suitable cabin air. But since the 1950s, most commercial planes have been redesigned to make cabin air by drawing in a compressed supply of it from plane engines. Typically, this so-called 'bleed air' is mixed with existing cabin air and re-circulated throughout the flight. The problem is that the area of the engine from which this air is drawn is often contaminated with toxic fumes from the friction that occurs between various moving parts and seals, and the oil that lubricates them. The seals are supposed to block fumes from getting into the cabin, but they are not 100 percent effective. And like everything else, they wear down over time, letting more and more oil mix with hot compressed air. Sometimes so much oil mixes with air entering the cabin that passengers and crew will literally be able to see fumes and smoke filling the cabin. This is referred to as a 'fume event'.

The type of oil used to lubricate plane engines[32, 33] is a complex, synthetic variety that has been specially formulated to endure extreme conditions. It is filled with all kinds of toxic components, including known neurotoxins that are also used in pesticides and nerve gas agents, called organophosphates. Organophosphates, similar to chemical agents produced during World War II, are some of the most common mass-produced chemicals assaulting human health today. Developed in Germany in the 1940s, these toxic compounds are responsible for a host of neurological disorders cropping up in modern society.

Simple inhalation, ingestion or skin contact may start the poisoning process. Not only do organophosphates disrupt the neurons in the body, but they also wreak havoc on the endocrine system. Especially, one compound is often mentioned in the media and documentaries in connection with Aerotoxic Syndrome: TCP (tricresyl phosphate). This we have to define properly, since TCP itself is not the only and not the worst neurotoxic agent, but its 'brother' TCoP, plus others.

TCP (and other components) are able to inhibit cholinesterase and it has been well known since 1930 that TCP is a neurotoxin when the tri-ortho isomer (ToCP)[21, 22, 23] was used to adulterate ethanol extracts of ginger and paralysed 10,000 to 50,000 individuals (Smith and Lillie, 1931; Parascandola, 1995). It can cause neurotoxic associated neuropathy.

One particular manufacturer's jet oil material safety data sheet/fact sheet states a clear warning. It says that the contained product, in this case they mention TCP clearly, can cause symptoms which are associated with cholinesterase inhibition; it can also produce neurotoxicity with the inhibition of neuropathy target esterase (NTE). It also states that effects of cholinesterase inhibition are expected to occur within hours of exposure, but, and this is interesting since it is so often denied by certain industry representatives, that neurotoxicity related to NTE inhibition might not become evident for several days – so this is a delayed reaction. Due to this some people will most likely not connect such reactions to the flight they were on the week before, and no one will be the wiser. The physicians will not know what they are looking for, the patient is feeling miserable, and will possibly, if the symptoms persist, be wrongly diagnosed and worse, medicated for something other than what their real problem is.

The warning can't be any clearer; at least this company is certainly not hiding the danger, whereas others try to by downplaying hazards, so why does the airline industry not pay any heed? However, it is interesting that on the JET OIL II EG German version safety data sheet, dated 4 July 2008, this specific warning was removed, or was it just – conveniently – forgotten?

It must be classified!

But why is there this media 'hype' about TCP and such a focus on this particular substance? The investigative journalist Tim van Beveren gave me the answer to that. When he worked on his first report on the subject, which was aired in February 2009 on German public TV station ARD, the editors decided to conduct their own testing on-board various aircraft, belonging to various airlines. In order to prove that engine oil residue was present within the aircraft cabins that were sampled, the journalists needed to focus on one specific compound that is present in the engine oil. "The TCP was the little finger of the right hand of our suspect", explained van Beveren. "Of course the suspect has nine more fingers, but, also out of cost considerations for the required analysis in a specialised lab, we focussed on what we knew at that time and it was TCP!" The other issue also had to do with costs and the availability of standards required in the lab to compare the samples, with the help of a gas chromatograph analysis. TCP is commonly available on the free market. Other compounds in the mixture are not and the oil-industry wasn't cooperating in identifying the individual compounds at all. "Also, the editors in their ambition to reduce complex matters to more simplification for a wide audience loved it. The bad guy had a name, 'TCP', and it was just three letters", explained van Beveren and added: "This was probably the biggest mistake made in the reporting, but unfortunately my careful warnings were ignored."

To me it is surprising that editors do not listen to their best researchers – the editors might as well invent their stories if they do not pay heed.

Can exposure to organophosphates make people sick?

The Department of Human Health, Centres for Disease Control and Prevention says that symptoms of a sudden poisoning with organophosphates can start during or after exposure, depending on how the poison has been in touch with the system (inhalation, skin contact, ingestion). Symptoms will start fastest after organophosphates are inhaled followed by eating or drinking them through contaminated food or water or getting them on your skin, for instance by aerosol spraying. Some of the symptoms that quickly appear are headache, dizziness, weakness, diarrhoea, nausea and vomiting, salivation and small pupils. Some people can react with very severe symptoms such as seizures, slow pulse, difficulty in breathing, and even fall into a coma. They state that long after exposure, people can also develop nervous system problems such as muscle weakness and numbness and tingling of the hands and feet (neuropathy). Something that the industry likes to deny.

Also, long-term exposure to organophosphates can cause confusion, anxiety, loss of memory, poor concentration, disorientation, balance problems, depression and personality changes, which some of our colleagues have reported, saying it was as if they were watching another person, and were unable to do anything about it (CDC-Gov)[11, 34, 35].

Other compounds

Heavy metal particles such as nickel, cadmium and beryllium and de-icing fluid can also make their way into the mix as the 'bleed air' is drawn through engine channels.

Because these various toxic compounds are exposed to extremely hot engine air, there's no telling what kinds of new contaminant cocktails are formed by the time this air enters the cabin. Scientists say that these 'cocktails' can be even more toxic and thus even more harmful than the single compounds.

You are probably aware that 'regular' air pollution, as you can encounter in huge cities, say Beijing, New York or Mexico City, affects your heart and lungs, but what about your brain? Like most environmental toxicants, air pollution does not discriminate in its targets… it hits your entire body, with effects on everything, from behaviour to brain health.

Particulate matter is air pollution made up of extremely small particles or liquid droplets called nano-particles – for more explanations on this technology I would read some of

Professor Jeremy Ramsden's[36] work or an attempt of an explanation in connection with aerotoxicity by me[37]. Typically, it's composed of any number of toxicants, including organic chemicals, metals, soil or dust. The smaller the diameter of the particle, the greater its risk of health damage becomes, as these can easily pass into your lungs, causing well-documented damage to your heart and lungs. 'Fine' particulate matter is generally defined as particles that are 2.5 micrometres or less. These particles may come from smoke, such as forest fires, as well as gases emitted from power plants, industries and cars. The US Environmental Protection Agency (EPA) considers any particles that are 10 micrometres or less as a potential health concern. Do your own maths.

There is growing evidence that fine particulate matter poses a risk to brain health and development. The IARC and WHO designate airborne particulates as Group 1 carcinogens. They say that such fine particulate matter may affect cognitive function by its harmful effects on the cardiovascular system – which is connected to the brain through blood vessels – and 'possibly by directly acting on the brain itself'[38].

'May' or 'can' – it's more of a 'does have' when one sees the many thousands who have health issues after exposure to these airborne particles. The following elaborates a bit on that.

Air Pollution Linked to Accelerated Memory Decline and Behaviour Problems

More and more scientists are stating that it is becoming increasingly clear that toxicants in the air we breathe may significantly damage our brains. The research suggests that air pollution may cause damage in both the early and late stages of life. One study even found that 'neurodegenerative disorders' (such as Alzheimer's) may begin early in life, with air pollutants playing a crucial role.

According to a German study presented at the EuroPRevent 2013 Congress in Rome, long-term exposure to fine particulate matter air pollution is associated with arthrosclerosis, or damage-induced thickening of the arteries.

Fine particle matter is believed to increase your cardiovascular disease risk by causing an imbalance in your autonomic nervous system (ANS), the part of your brain that is intricately involved in regulating biological functions such as blood pressure, blood sugar levels, clotting, and viscosity. There are actually quite a few mechanisms by which air pollution harms both your heart and your brain.

One might ask the question: Is it legal to allow the ingestion of brain altering chemicals? Surely this cannot be categorised as good practice for the general public and the entire planet?

It is known that exposure to one type of air pollution, ozone, may trigger inflammation of your vascular system, increasing risk factors associated with heart disease. Ozone exposure has also been linked to a change in heart rate variability and a reduction in the ability of blood clots to dissolve, both of which can lead to heart problems and potentially stroke. Doesn't the brain send signals to the heart and cells? So if those signals are impaired due to toxic damage, what happens?

The mould allergy I spoke of earlier is often the end result of constant exposure to mould of a toxic substance. A common misconception among allergologists who are not trained in this type of toxic compound, which is technically not their area of expertise unless they have trained specifically in environmental medicine, with their background in immunology and neurology is, to do general allergen testing followed by desensitisation shots[39]. Been there, done that.

Common symptoms that can be attributed to toxic indoor air quality include:

- Headaches
- Dizziness
- Balance Problems
- Brain Fog

- Vision Problems
- Fatigue and Lethargy
- Depression
- Aggression
- Allergies
- Poor Concentration and Forgetfulness
- Word Finding Problems
- Rashes
- Stomach and Digestive Problems
- Breathing Problems
- Muscle Weakness
- Muscle Pain
- Sciatic Pain (toxic pain)
- Hair Loss
- Neurological Problems
- Tremor
- Tinnitus
- Loss of Hearing
- Endocrine Imbalances (thyroid, fertility)

The most effective way to improve your air quality, starting at home, is to control or, better, eliminate as many sources of pollution as you can first, before using any type of air purifier, if any.

This includes accounting for moulds, tobacco smoke, volatile organic compounds from paints, aerosol sprays and household cleaners, pesticides, phthalates from vinyl flooring and personal care products; pollutants from pressure-treated wood products, radon gas, glues from wall to wall carpets or wood flooring, carpets treated with flame retardants and pesticides and more. And be aware of mould anywhere, your bathroom, kitchen, room corners and cellar – all are prone to mould contamination if not well insulated, heated and aired.

But how do you avoid them on an airplane? There are many toxic agents on airplanes, some of which you might not even be aware. And that's where you spend a lot of your time!

Toxic Fumes

Toxic flame-retardant chemicals for instance are widely used in furniture cushions filled with foam, woollen and synthetic fibre carpets, the material they are covered with, in foam insulation, in practically everything you can think of, despite research showing they may cause neurodevelopment issues, even cancer, and endocrine problems such as fertility and thyroid imbalances.

Astonishingly, fact is that these chemicals seem to do little to actually suppress flames, which has been proven in comparison with untreated items. Some may even, due to the chemical reaction during a fire, increase the toxicity of the gasses it produces.

It seems that many studies have proven that flame-retardant chemicals are highly toxic, whether they're on fire or not; also these chemicals don't stay in the treated product, but migrate out, and collect in house, and other dust, which we inhale as well. I had a laboratory test done after taking a dust sample from an aircraft I worked on, and there they were, some of the unwanted chemicals.

What I never knew is that when an object treated with flame-retardant chemicals catches fire it will give off higher levels of toxic carbon monoxide, soot and smoke than an untreated object. So on board you have chemically treated carpets, passenger seats (leather or other material and the foam inside) and insulation in the walls of the aircraft, to name just a few. And a fire on board an aircraft is the one thing you do not want! Never mind the fact that the smoke hoods for the firefighting crew are not 100 percent secure, and do not last for longer than 20-30 minutes of protection.

And what about those aerosol sprays used for disinsection before landing in certain countries?

Prevention of airport malaria is based on aircraft disinsection for aircraft coming from malaria endemic areas. This disinsection is part of the International Health Regulations and must be done following the World Health Organisation's recommendations on disinsecting aircrafts. Several methods are available. Either the 'blocks away' procedure, which means spraying before take-off, while passengers are already on board, and doors are closed. Or pre-flight and top of descent, which is spraying before passengers come on board, and/or spraying a fast acting insecticide during the flight just as it starts descent for landing. And the third possibility is the residual treatment, which means that the entire internal surface of the aircraft, cabin and hold, is sprayed on a regular basis.

Airlines can choose between these methods. For the two first methods, health authorities of the arrival airport ask for the presentation of empty aerosol dispensers as evidence of disinsection. For the third method, airlines must show a disinsection certificate given by a legal authority as evidence of compliance to disinsection regulations.

Many reports completed by flight attendants or airline personnel suggest the possibility of the onset of symptoms in passengers and crewmembers consequent to pyrethroid application. The reported symptoms vary from irritation of eyes, throat and upper respiratory tract and, in some cases, skin irritation, to severe respiratory symptoms such as dyspnoea, cough and even asthma. In many cases, flu-like symptoms, such as sore muscles, headaches and allergic reactions were reported. All of which I experienced.

Like other chemicals, insecticides used in aircraft disinsection have the potential to cause a wide range of toxic effects. If it can kill bugs within seconds, what makes anyone believe it can do no harm in larger animals or human beings?

According to Dr Don Weston (Integrative Biology, University of California, Berkely) who has been studying the environmental effects of pyrethroid insecticides since 2004, "Pyrethroids are very sticky and they don't like to be dissolved in the water – but it takes so little in the water to be toxic – only two parts per trillion." You need to be aware of the fact that you are always in contact with some residue sticking to the surfaces in the aircraft. So you get it on your fingers, hands, on your clothes and of course you inhale it.

In my case even DDT was found, which dumbfounded my physician at the time. A worldwide ban on its agricultural use was formalised under the Stockholm Convention (1972), but its limited use in disease vector control continues to this day and remains controversial. Any questions?

DDT caused hyperthyroidism at low dose rates and hypothyroidism at high dose rates in pigeons. Thus, the bone growth retardation in pesticide-treated broiler chicks may be influenced by disturbances in synthesis and secretion of growth hormone, thyroid hormone and glucocorticoids (Jeffries D.J. and French M.C. about DDT connected to hyper- or hypo-thyroidism in birds; 1969, 1971).

So again I ask, how can they say it is not harmful to human beings? Testing on animals will never give any form of accurate data on how something reacts in a human being. And who is crazy enough, including the scientists, to let themselves be used as guinea pigs for these toxic agents? Would you?

Toxicity test data are usually available only for pure substances, that are for the active ingredients or solvents used in insecticide formulations rather than for the pesticide formulations themselves. This applies also for the jet engine oil ingredients.

A permethrin (remember the insecticide I mentioned earlier which is present in the aerosol sprays for disinsection?) fact sheet states that the inhalation of the substance may cause headaches, nasal and respiratory irritation, difficulty in breathing, dizziness, nausea or vomiting.

Wet Dogs and Smelly Socks

An Explanation

The unpleasant smell of wet dog, vomit or smelly socks comes from a chemical reaction, which produces it.

Forensic investigators often identify the presence of poisons by their smells. For instance arsenic has a garlic-like smell, and hydrogen cyanide smells mildly of bitter almonds. Unfortunately not all poisons have a pleasant odour. Carbon monoxide is a notorious example. Many deaths from the gas occur because people cannot smell it while it's building up around them.

One of many examples reported in the media:

"A US Airways Boeing 767 plane where 15 people got sick, January 16 had been taken out of service twice in recent weeks for a foul odor... Maintenance logs obtained by News Channel 36 show the plane – tail number 0251 – experienced a similar problem on Dec 28 and Dec 30 on flights to San Juan, Puerto Rico. One note in the report reads, when thrust levers were reduced to idle for inital desent [sic] a very strong odor smelling like wet sox [sic] and/or dirty feet circulated through the pass. cabin and flt deck... Mechanics determined that the problem was a leak of the hydraulic fluid Skydrol."
(From wcnc.com jan.20.2010
www.wcnc.com/story/news/local/2014/06/19/10938105/)

I cannot tell you which compounds or mixture thereof exactly create these smells on board an aircraft since the oil manufacturers reserve the right to keep all other components of the oils a so-called trade secret, not disclosable to anyone but a select few on a need-to-know basis and then only after a non-disclosure agreement is signed. They are only obliged to disclose them upon a court order, say perhaps medical grounds. I have heard through the grapevine that plans may be in process to add odour-killing chemicals to the jet engine oils, which would mean? Nobody could smell toxic fumes anymore. This is in direct opposition (if true) to the fact that researchers came up with the idea of spiking noxious gasses (e.g. sarin) with smelly compounds; like natural gas, a potentially dangerous odourless agent can be spiked with minute concentrations of a highly smelly additive which will warn from imminent danger.

Now I am not a lawyer, but... I wonder if doing the opposite: by covering up smells from toxic gasses to avoid the potentially dangerous and, due to the smell, obvious pollution which warns of danger, if that were legal? If it were true.

But wait there's more, of which you will learn later on.

Tests after Exposure

The best way to go is to establish if you indeed are full of toxic material in connection with contaminated cabin air. I suggest having tests run as described in the following. If you had a very obvious exposure do not hesitate, get your bloods taken ASAP and take them home with you, and put them in the fridge and get in touch with e.g. Aerotoxic Association, Aerotoxic Team or ProHealth Medical immediately! I am saying this because we have experienced too many disappearances of blood samples in the past. Also, store a urine sample in the freezer if you can't get to the test kit fast enough. Remember, even if you don't smell or see fumes, you can still have been exposed, especially if you are experiencing the aforementioned symptoms while still on board or shortly after, or have been exposed to long-term low-level contamination which could be causing symptoms and recent health problems for which you haven't received any explanation. Additionally, I would also have them run tests for pesticides (best to do those that are listed on the aerosol sprays in the cans you use on board).

I am sure there are also other laboratories able to do many of the tests, but to date it is ProHealth Laboratory in The Netherlands as a fully independent organisation, and by working together with similar labs in Belgium, Luxemburg, Germany and the US, that has all current tests available due to their well-organised laboratory and their worldwide connections.

The aircraft cabin air tests they offer are intended to provide insight into whether a person was exposed to particular neurotoxic constituents of engine oil smoke/fumes on an aircraft. Options include an air sampler card and air pump/filter equipment, as well as a post-incident garment analysis. The blood tests offered may provide insight into whether a person is especially susceptible to the effects of certain neurotoxic constituents of the engine oil fumes, and whether there is objective evidence of damage to the central nervous system. The presence of TCPs also implies the presence of many other chemical compounds in oil fumes, many of which are carcinogenic and/or toxic. It should be noted that there are only very few occupational or public health exposure limits, either for individual constituents of engine oil fumes or for chemical mixtures in oil fumes.

Thus, the cabin air tests are an important tool to confirm exposure to oil fumes in the absence of other evidence. With kind permission by ProHealth's Mr Scheepers I cite the following from their programme:

Glial Auto-Antibodies Blood Test[24]

This is a test developed by Professor Abou Donia, which provides objective evidence of damage to the central and peripheral nervous systems, without the need for brain imaging and spinal tap. Although this test does not elucidate the cause of nervous system damage, it does confirm the damage from organophosphate poisoning, which can be helpful.

ToCP blood test is still under development and not yet available.

Cabin Air Tests

This is a very handy thing: you can get a SamplerCard®, the size of a post card, to detect the presence of TCPs. You place the card in the direct air current of a ventilation opening, for example on the hook of your chair in front of you, or in the galley. Or the sampling pump, which I used on my flight back to Ireland. It is a calibrated air-sampling pump with a filter to estimate the average concentration of airborne TCPs in the cabin or cockpit during the sampling period.

The airline tried to undermine this in my pre-court documentation, saying that the air-sampling pump I used, in their opinion, had not been used 'professionally' and was not validated. I say they were very worried and couldn't prove the opposite.

ProHealth also has possibilities to test TCP in white material (shirts). Coloured shirts are not to be used because of the dyes, which interfere in the test.

The urine tests for TCP metabolites have to be taken within 24 hours after returning from a flight. At this moment they have three packages to test the urine:

1. TCP metabolites in morning urine.
2. Organophosphates metabolites in morning urine.
3. Chemical metabolites from oil and other compounds in morning urine.

Micro-nutrients

Before taking vitamins and minerals you should get your levels tested, to make sure you are as a matter of fact lacking them. This would apply in my opinion e.g. for selenium, glutathione, vitamin D, zinc, and magnesium. Possibly also the vitamin B-range.

A complete medical check based on blood, urine and saliva tests can be done and due to the fact that ProHealth Medical has a comprehensive range of test protocols, they can provide pilots, crew and of course passengers with an extensive check-up.

AChE (within 24 hours)

An acute poisoning is when you have just been exposed to and have inhaled strong smells or even smoke from a fume event on a particular flight.

Acetylcholinesterase hydrolyses the neurotransmitter, acetylcholine, at neuromuscular junctions and brain cholinergic synapses, and thus terminates signal transmission. It is the primary target by organophosphorus compounds such as nerve agents and pesticides. Organophosphates (OP), esters of phosphoric acid, are a class of irreversible AChE inhibitors. Irreversible AChE inhibitors are/have been used in insecticides and nerve gases for chemical warfare.

This requires a specific device, which is not always available immediately – yet. In The Netherlands it is, via Dr Michel Mulder, and I believe very soon via ProHealth Medical Laboratory[7].

You could get the following tests done elsewhere:

Hair Analysis

Hair analysis testing is another possibility and gives a complete picture of a person's health history. A hair analysis can also be a guide to mineral deficiencies and if heavy metal toxicity may be a concern. A hair analysis test can also be an overall indicator of antioxidant and vitamin needs. If toxins are high, it indicates antioxidants are low. Hair analysis testing would be helpful to identify specifically what nutrients your body needs for optimal physical, emotional health and wellness. Just taking a general multi-vitamin/mineral complex may not be what your body needs.

When Toxins Attack the Nerves

Frank Cannon, lawyer in the well-documented case of a pilot's premature death, which was brought in connection with contaminated cockpit air says: "Also very important is the issue of genetic variability between individuals", and that some people have a DNA coding that means they lack the necessary enzymes to detoxify properly or at all.

He continues: "The rule emerges that if you are unable to detoxify between flights at a rate, which is equal to or greater than the rate at which you are re-intoxicated by repetitive, successive and cumulative exposures, you will become extremely unwell." This is what applied to me.

"Minimum safety levels are a fallacy, with no known basis", he said. "Real neurotoxic injury is caused by long-term low-level exposure. When a plane lands, the passengers get off, but the crew turn around and do the same thing all over again, day in day out."

There are indications that even if there are no acute symptoms, exposure to organophosphates at low levels, which is constantly being denied by the industry as not being possible, can cause central nervous system effects and even severe damage, as several human studies have found out in nerve conduction and neuropsychiatry problems (Christopher M. Morris et al[40]).

The thing is, that faced with a huge number of compounds to be tested, toxicologists tend to streamline their processes to reduce the number of animals they use and the number of doses per experiment. A typical toxicological examination derives study-specific LOAELs (lowest observed adverse effect levels) and NOAEL (no observed adverse effect levels)[41] from experimental data in which they use animal models and in which only 2-4 different doses of the compound are actually under scrutiny. With the goal of deriving a NOAEL with only a few doses, it becomes immediately clear that any insight into what is happening in the domain below the NOAEL really cannot be achieved by such restricted studies. Even a layman can see that it takes many more doses, time and sadly animals, to get a clear picture of what biological responses happen to low exposures of certain toxins (and over a long term). Never mind the fact that they are testing on helpless animals and not on humans that in my opinion cannot be the same thing, on top of not taking into consideration that one person reacts differently to another.

With that in mind you have good legs to stand on if someone tells you long-term low-dose cannot be a problem. How do they know? Ask them to prove it.

First do no Harm

Most scientists and physicians would rather not wait until there is a diagnosable disease to address the underlying problems that, over time, cause the signs and symptoms that influence the development of illness and disease.

Symptoms one experiences from a poisoning can lead to a false diagnosis, as we have seen with many flight crews who were mistakenly diagnosed with e.g. Parkinson's disease.

Returning a patient's health requires reversing (or substantially improving) the specific dysfunctions that have contributed to the disease state. Those dysfunctions are the result of lifelong interactions among our environmental exposures, our lifestyle influences, and often also our genetic predispositions.

Genetic predispositions are a major factor in how a person's immune system can or cannot detox properly. Not only in our case. We must bear in mind that our bodies are not made to digest, metabolise or detox SYNTHETIC materials!

It is of the essence that help-seekers who think they may have an aerotoxic injury with resulting health issues look for a medical health practitioner who is experienced in toxicology and neurology, and if possible has some formal education in Orthomolecular Medicine, Functional Medicine or Naturopathy.

Why? Because it is essential that the symptoms are recognised as acute, or after-effects, and are the result of a poisoning. It is also important that they are aware of and don't dismiss 'long-term low-level' (LTLL) exposure to neurotoxic agents as a possibility, rather than rush to conclusions and diagnose them as being symptoms from an illness with a fancy name!

The subjects that should be looked into are:

- Digestion, Absorption, Respiration;
- Exposure Sources, Toxicity, Detoxification;
- Endocrine, Neurotransmitters, Immune Messengers;
- Immune, Inflammation, Infection;
- Energy Regulation, Mitochondrial Function;
- Sub-cellular Membranes, Musculoskeletal Integrity;
- Cardiovascular and Lymphatic Systems.

Before we move into the part where I share with you how you could help yourself detox and rebuild your cellular health and get your energy back, let me tell you about the legal case. Again I had been without warning exposed to and injured by toxic cabin air, and not only I thought it was my given right to receive compensation, never mind an apology. This is what happened.

Justice will be served?

The law requires employers to provide their employees with working conditions that are free of known dangers. Workers have a right to a safe workplace. Well, we know how that ended for many others and me. What about passengers? *"The carrier shall be liable for damage sustained in the event of the death or wounding of a passenger or any other bodily injury suffered by a passenger, if the accident which caused the damage so sustained took place on board the aircraft or in the course of any operations of embarking or disembarking."*

The professional opinion and expertise of several of the top professionals in the field of Aerotoxic Injury/Syndrome was that it was a sure case of in-flight personal injury (according to the Montreal Convention, Passengers' Rights). Also, the lawyer I hired thought so.

I gathered tons of information that I kept forwarding to my young lawyer, of whom I thought had the necessary guts and stamina. I intended to help her be well informed on a yet unknown subject. She advised me to get several expert opinions, independent if possible, to strengthen the case and 'for the judge to understand' and, she said, I needed to advise those experts that they would have to present in person.

All had to be paid out of my pocket. Of course, all the experts came from different parts of the world: USA, England, The Netherlands and Germany, which increased the amount of expenses.

I got it all done, looking at a bill of around 15,000 Euros, without the lawyer and barrister's fees.

As time went on, the closer the court hearing date came and the more expert opinions I got, the more my lawyer was telling me they were not enough or not good enough. Suddenly, after a conference call with him, my experts and I were informed that the barrister was putting the case down. Then I had one of my episodes and was very ill. I was so weak and physically off-balance I once again had to support myself with a cane to get around. I requested a postponement of the set date on grounds of ill health. The judge declined this although I had sent her recommendations from three medical experts that I was unable to travel. She virtually indicated that she didn't believe it, since such a request had been submitted once before, because one of my lead experts had been taken seriously ill two weeks before the initial hearing date and she ordered me to come 'by hook or by crook' or risk being in contempt of court! What?

My lawyer was not good at helping me with that one, shrugging her shoulders, so I instructed her to get a new barrister. What was going on? The next one barely looked at the case, sent me a bill for 700 Euros and declined, saying he did not have time. I was advised to let it go. Without telling me why, just a general: it is not a strong case.

After all those expert opinions and material they had? I noticed that she was evading my questions; she ignored some or neglected to answer others. She was not well informed; in a meeting about four weeks before the hearing, I realised that she didn't know what she was talking about, even her superior noticed, but of course said nothing. She clearly had never looked at any of the material I had sent her, and had not read the expert opinions I presented. In short she was not interested; she was not acting for me, her client, as she should have. All my supporting friends and experts were completely exasperated with her and the way she was (not) handling things. She was treating the case as if it were a simple open and shut case of a broken leg after slipping on a wet floor in a supermarket. I requested someone different, but she was left on the case, supported by someone slightly senior to her and there was no time left to find a new law firm.

It had become close to impossible to discuss important business with her in the meantime, each meeting ended in unpleasantness. I was losing trust in her, and was beginning to have huge doubts. Was she on the receiving end of 'brown envelopes'? There was an incident and a comment or two, which made me think so! One day she called me, sounding excited, saying she just got a fax from the defendant's lawyer indicating that they wanted to talk. A few hours later an email arrived saying: It was a mistake, the defendant's secretary made a mistake, it was a different case, different person, wrong name, wrong date, wrong everything... ah, really? Hardly.

The third barrister came and went... and we were still waiting for a specific document after our repeated request for disclosure by the airline, which in the end we never received, because my lawyer was incapable of getting it. Or was she?

Just two weeks before the hearing she found another barrister who took the case. But of course he was under huge pressure to read into it. On October 16th 2010 we, that is Tim van Beveren, the investigative journalist who had been working and regularly reporting on the subject for the past six years, and a staff editor from a German TV station, flew with me on-board this airline involved, to Dublin. The camera crew arrived the next day and they took pictures and interviewed the experts and me over the next four days. We were at the courthouse on time – 10am. We were listed first on the board to be heard by the judge. The barrister came back from the general court meeting of all present solicitors, barristers and the presiding judge. "There's a problem", he said. "There is no judge." Puzzled, we looked at each other, and then burst out laughing because we thought it was a joke. It wasn't.

Half an hour, then one hour later, still no judge. No explanation. "Go back to the hotel", said the barrister, adding that he would call us when a judge was ready.

The call came to be there at 3pm. No, we were not to be heard, another case was brought in, which was listed number four or five after us. But, he said he had located the defendant's barrister and intended 'to have a chat over coffee with him'.

Day Two. My barrister was still speaking with the defendant's. A first hint of a possible out of court settlement was indicated. The amount? Not sure.

Then it was revoked. A few hours later an offer was 'sort of' made but not confirmed. Interestingly though, the amount they didn't mention, didn't go up, it came down, not even indicating any numbers, just saying it won't be as much as previously hinted at!

This went back and forth the entire day, and still no judge for us. The possible settlement sum without numbers came downhill all the time.

Day Three. The same. No judge. Talk went back and forth, and then the final spectacular offer came; they stated: "You will lose the case anyway, but we will be generous. We will not charge you our expenses but there will also be no settlement." And furthermore they said: "If you don't take this most generous offer, we will send you our full legal bill which will amount to about 120,000 Euros, and sue you if you don't pay up."

Was I supposed to accept that?

My barrister, from under his shock of pure white hair, looked at me over the rim of his reading glasses, waiting for my reply.

Leaning on my cane, I raised my eyebrows and said one word: "No."

Expecting nothing else he didn't say a word, just whisked off, black robes flying, to convey the message and seek a new date.

Some weeks later I was given a new date by the court, no apologies of course, but the judge insisted, although otherwise requested, that I must bring all experts again, and make sure that they could stay more than the scheduled four to five days. She refused to allow video conferencing, which would have been feasible for the experts, time and expense-wise and me. So I was looking at another at least 10,000 to 12,000 Euros. I couldn't afford it, and after many sleepless nights, I withdrew. Something I hated doing!

My solicitor had requested for me to sign a Notice of Discharge just two weeks before that, so I was without a brief anyway and to find a new one was more than I could handle in such a short time and after the experience with her and the barristers. She had mentioned a sum for her fee though: 60-70,000 Euros. But without any ado she waived that in the end...

I wonder?

If I had had the money I would have never given up!

I would have won in the end, I know, I would have. The evidence is mounting every day as I write, and it would have supported my case.

Also quite remarkable in this context is the fact that the German public TV station decided a few months later that my case would not be part of their reporting. I was told by one of the staff editors that they had given preference to the case of another victim, which in the end didn't appear either in what was broadcast in July 2014. I then learned that apparently my former employer declined to give an interview to the station because of a picture they claim they found on the Internet. It was the picture of me on board the flight to Dublin that Tim van Beveren took with my permission after he had informed the cabin staff about his intentions to do so, and nobody objected. The station later claimed that Tim van Beveren committed a 'journalistic misdemeanour' when he posted this picture early in 2014 on his private Facebook page, where he was communicating with other affected victims since he started working on this documentary in January 2013. In the end, van Beveren was no longer author of his film and something I would term as a 'soft-wash' was finally aired, but only after being re-edited by a senior editor of the station and without any further involvement of the investigative journalist, or his former co-author. All coincidental? Who knows?

To date, legal cases like mine on contaminated cabin air have not been very successful at all, or were classified and kept well under the radar when out of court settlements were made – possibly accompanied by a gagging order or, one case filed by a flight attendant took eighteen years to finally be settled. Passengers have won a couple of cases in connection with the aerosol pesticide spraying though. A passenger had a life-threatening asthma attack in an airplane triggered by the spraying of the disinsectant permethrin in 2011 and received a settlement from that airline. But settlements won't be enough. Too often the airlines get away with it, as happened in my case, because of clueless or gullible lawyers or when the money runs out – they have endless funds; sick people don't.

Many people's health is ruined for life. The aviation industry must make the necessary changes to their equipment, and stop their endless denial of something that is as clear as crystal. Boeing has proven it can be done with their Boeing 787 Dreamliner, although they won't admit they made the changes to avoid bleed air – one could question why they did it, if there are no reasons for worries about contaminated cabin air in the first place – so why are they and other aircraft manufacturers not building all newly-ordered airplanes just like that? Also, engine oil must be developed that does not contain such toxic material, as I believe at least one company has already offered. It is hard to believe that those oils aren't good enough.

In addition, the use of toxic compounds in interior, airtight places, altogether, and every country's regulations regarding the disinsectant spraying of highly toxic insecticides must be reviewed.

WHO must stop their policy of making rules and then creating loopholes, giving options for exceptions. Scientists and the medical profession must acknowledge that long-term low-level exposure to neurotoxic chemicals can be as health and life threatening as a single exposure to VOC (volatile organic compound) spraying, or a visible fume event engulfing everybody on board in toxic smoke. Not the best of academics can know for sure who is more or less susceptible than others. Side effects and resulting symptoms are those effects that accompany a chemical or medicine's use. The industry admits that they expect them in a certain percentage of the population. So why deny that there is a certain percentage of crew and passengers who have serious side effects to chemicals they are inhaling unknowingly, involuntarily and without prescription? Of course they would have to admit first that the contamination exists. It is a game of Russian roulette that is being played with people's health and wellbeing. It is a serious breach of respect toward employees and paying customers and their health.

I received dozens of emails from affected pilots and cabin crew of whom some are involved in court cases as I write. They sent me copies of their flight reports as well as medical reports. Flight reports are written when certain incidences on board an aircraft happen. All of them report fumes, smells and incapacitation of the cockpit crew for moments or the remainder of the flight and after. All medical reports give evidence of the presence of jet engine oil contaminants in their bloods. How did they get there?

Testimonies by Aerotoxic Sufferers

1. "I am just one of many. One who has suffered severe poisoning from contaminated cabin air. From many years

of experience in dealing with poisoned cockpit, and cabin crew, as well as getting to know passengers, who display typical toxicological symptoms on or after a flight.

"I know that there are many like me. I was lucky that, after many years of odyssey, I met very competent and impartial expert Professor Helmuth Müller-Mohnssen. Without him, who was a courageous environmental health expert, I would have certainly died from the effects of multiple nerve poisons I was exposed to during my eleven years of service as a flight attendant. Professor Müller-Mohnssen, the most knowledgeable nerve toxin and pesticide expert, was one of the world's best scientists in diagnosing a poisoning by nerve agents. I spent months visiting doctors and spending unnecessary time in hospitals for surgeries, diagnostics and ineffective treatment methods. Toxicological evaluation criteria were all simply ignored by attending physicians and flight medics. Doctors, who despite the severity and the typical toxicological symptoms did not even consider them, subjected me to daily pain and indignities. Instead they shocked me over and over with false diagnoses, such as multiple sclerosis and rheumatism or with prophecies that in no later than 2 years I would die. In 1999, my eleven-year career at Lufthansa, with increasingly occurring long-term illnesses, came to an end and I was declared unfit to fly by my company's flight medic. Despite better knowledge he did not confirm the diagnosis of severe poisoning and tried to falsify the diagnosis. Ever since I have been fighting for a disability compensation and I try to help others with the same predicament." (Aida Infante, former purser)

2. Another sick aviator who wished to remain anonymous:

   "Bio monitoring measurements have shown the presence of substances at a six to fifteen times higher rate, in excess of daily exposure and higher than the corresponding official values (MAK maximum workplace concentration) allow. However, these control measurements by MAK are not relevant for us on a public carrier (aircraft) since they were devised for workers in a high hazard workplace environment, who wear protective gear including full face breathing protection, which we do not. Limits or standards for indoor air for these substances do not exist because they (substances) are far too toxic to be allowed indoor; never mind in a hermetically sealed tin (aircraft)

"If [name of institute and airline withheld] conduct measurements and analyse exclusively on the basis of indoor air issues according to and for public transport, it is no surprise if they find no significant abnormalities, because they would not be looking for them. [Author: Remember what I said earlier in the book? One has to point a finger for e.g. laboratories to search for the right substance.]

"Already an estimated 50 percent of colleagues have trouble with significant peripheral neurological complaints, such as tingling in the fingers, feet, etc., but remain without receiving explanations relating to a possible toxin exposure at work..." (Name known to author.)

3. Case history of sicknesses by a flight attendant who wishes to stay anonymous:

   "Since the beginning of my work as an airhostess I have had episodes of a kind of migraine every four to eight weeks. Then I started the day with headaches, which became stronger during the day. In the afternoon hours or evening I started vomiting – often more than 10 times. Usually I had this for one day. During 2013 and 2014 these episodes lasted several days. But after my last flight in 2014 I did not vomit again. Two to three times a year I had a bad cold.

   "In the summer of 2013 my husband and I spent a short vacation of four or five days at the Baltic Sea. One evening I visited the sauna. I swam a short round in the natural pool they had. I was about to get out but suddenly my body had a mind of its own and threw itself to the left and went under the surface without me being able to control it. I didn't understand at all what was happening in this moment. I fought with my body to get out of there, which was actually an area where I could even stand. But my body did not listen to me and continued to go back to the left and under the surface although stairs were in front of me, I could not get to them. I could not shout or do anything like it. I was lucky – there was a couple sitting not far from where I was. The lady realised that something was wrong with me and sent her husband who pulled me out of the pool, otherwise I would have drowned. As suddenly as my body function had gone to not normal it changed back to normal. So far I had no idea what this was all about.

"One day after that summer in 2013 my alarm clock rang. I looked at it – it was spinning around and around and around at a very high speed. About half an hour later the haunting was over.

"I used to go jogging from time to time – not too fast or too long. One day I could not stop anymore but became faster and faster instead. So I decided to will myself to fall down at a certain point as the only way of a 'controlled' stop.

"In October 2013 I got strong convulsions in my legs and arms. I stopped working for three months. Suddenly I had extra systoles in the heart and a short but strong headache after drinking simple water. At the end of January I felt better.

"I had an MRI of the head done in October 2013. 'Hydrocephalus' was diagnosed. I wondered about that because I knew this from children being born with it. In January I asked the company's aviation medical examiner if the doctor who diagnosed me was wrong. And the examiner said yes that this diagnose could not be the right one. Later the convulsions disappeared.

"At the end of February I had a very severe cold. I had a retraining on big aircraft in Frankfurt. I only had about six or seven flight days until the 10th April.

"Then I had a four or five day's rotation – my last one on an aircraft. On 14th April we landed in Tel Aviv. I wanted to switch door 1L [first left door front] of an A321 into 'park' position. But suddenly the convulsions were back. I looked at the door and couldn't find the slide handle nor the door handle because everything was white, a big white area in front of my eyes. I turned around in order to go into the cockpit. I looked up to punch in the code but I could not remember it in this moment – after 11 years of flying in the position that placed me at this door, 1L. I also could not remember the telephone number to call the cockpit. I turned back to the door and scanned the door with my hands and hoped to find the handles this way. But I was not successful. The pilots were watching me via cameras. This was the moment for our captain to come out of the cockpit. She sent me into the cockpit. I was not aware of any passengers waiting in the galley. After about half an hour I was quite normal again.

"Next day I went home. During the following weeks and months symptoms worsened. In July I could hardly walk, my short-term memory had nearly gone, my thinking had been slowed down very much and I could hardly speak. In my mind I could only find pictures of my childhood, songs of my childhood and so on. Sitting on the couch I let myself fall on the left side without being aware of it. The muscles in my face went slack. Mentally and physically I was handicapped. Within myself I could think but only there. I often fell and lost consciousness for a few seconds. I found out that I didn't tolerate coffee anymore. From a friend I got strong enzymes that had been fermented over three and a half years. Three weeks after starting to take them I 'came back'. Today I can walk nearly normal again, I speak normal and the extra systoles in the heart are much less. But often I feel weak, very tired and have strange headaches. Also my legs become tired from time to time. I had three more MRI investigations. The doctors looked for a tumour but could not find any. They spoke about surgery but finally the surgeon said that it is not necessary when I feel like I do now. It would be too risky. I asked him what he wanted to take out of the head if there is no tumour to be found. He did not answer. One doctor who already took part in the autopsies of pilots and flight attendants said that there is damaged brain tissue in my head. The organophosphates in the air of aircraft may trigger an autoimmune disease leading to damaged brain tissue.

"My medicine mainly is: linseed oil, coconut oil, MSM, vitamin C, OPC, seeds of stinging nettle and volcano powder. I guess it will take more time to get rid of the remaining symptoms like muscle weakness, headaches, kind of rushing in the ears like being at the ocean, the dizziness and all the other symptoms showing up from time to time.

"I spoke with my boss and talked to the airline doctors. The boss said that so many colleagues don't have the problems I have. I told him that so many colleagues don't have the problems I have but other major health problems. One airline doctor even yelled at me, how I could spend money on blood investigations by Professor Abou Donia? Though he did not speak of 'Professor' but disrespectfully as of a postgraduate whom he would have thrown out because this postgraduate according to him had not done any scientific work…" (Name withheld)

4. Another flight attendant

"I am 44 years old and have been employed since 2000 at a large German airline as cabin staff. In summer of 2013, I experienced within two months, two so-called 'fume events', the second with no real smell. In June 2013, a colleague mentioned on a flight from Frankfurt to Berlin an acrid smell at the door of an A321. The captain asked me to check it. I also noticed the smell immediately. Within a few minutes I felt dizzy, got a headache, felt nauseous, with severe abdominal pain, a strong metallic taste and tingling in my hands and certain disorientation. I was barely able to equip our new pots and anyone who has already done this, knows that it is not an intellectual achievement. The colleague at door No. 2 had not been in the rear section of the plane, and she was still good, so she took over my duties. After landing, two colleagues and I were taken to the hospital. I had an exceptionally high blood pressure. In the hospital we were observed for 24 hours and then released. In the urine they nothing was found [surprise!]. Even the medical service of my employer found no exceptional values. In the following weeks how I felt went in waves but uphill. After 5 weeks, I reported back for duty. However, a slight dizziness and nausea accompanied my daily life.

"In August 2013 I was re-contaminated on a flight. On board I noticed in myself and other colleagues increasing fatigue, headaches and lack of concentration, but no abnormal smell was noticeable. On the way home, which I can hardly remember, I arrived home and fell into a state of delirium, I literally collapsed. In the following days I still could not concentrate more than only a few minutes at a time. After two days, my partner said, I had to do something because 'with your eyes closed, you look as if you had just died'. The next three days I spent in a professional hospital. Again, no exceptional values were found, only the oxygen saturation of the blood was slightly below average. I suffered from severe dizziness, visual and audio effects, numb fingers, absolute lack of libido, insomnia, neck pain, headaches and nausea. A state which did not improve for a long time. Three days later an environmental doctor who knew immediately what was wrong took care of me, but too much time had now elapsed to find plane typical poisons, however, there was a high concentration of insecticides found with which aircraft are regularly treated.

"Until this summer, I was a sports enthusiast, after these incidents I could hardly get up the stairs. Many detoxifications later and a total avoidance and contact with chemicals such as fragrances, etc., it has taken about 1.5 years in waves to slowly come uphill, and a significant improvement in my condition has taken place. But to date nothing has really changed in the visual effects; I still have a tunnel vision as after excessive alcohol consumption, the tinnitus has remained the right more than left. Some days I have strong muscle twitches in different body areas, almost all joints ache sometimes. The vertigo is weaker, but still noticeable. My memory performance has improved significantly, but is still below average.

"Before I got sick, I had taken heed of the issue of contaminated cabin air only in passing, and had imagined it to happen about as frequently or rarely as a plane crash. Looking back, I certainly had suffered in previous years already from significant toxicity. Permanent respiratory problems, frequent headaches during or after the flights, nausea on board, insomnia at home and during the layover etc. In 2012 I was hospitalised due to severe vertigo, which was then dubbed after diagnosis of exclusion, as neuritis vestibularis, today I rather suspect that it was also a result of contaminated cabin air." (Anonymous, name known)

5. And another flight attendant's story:

   "We were flying from Frankfurt to San Francisco. During take-off we noticed a weird smell. We did not know what it was but it was so bad I was only able to breathe through my blouse, holding the collar up to my nose. My throat and my nose were burning. Not even the cockpit knew what it was and they called the engineers on the ground. The engineers told us that they cleaned one of the engines and that everything should be all right again if this engine would not provide the cabin with air any more. The cockpit did as they were told. They shut the engine off from providing the cabin with air.

   "Me and my colleagues were not sure if we just got accustomed to the smell or if it vanished. I was able to breathe normal again and my throat and nose stopped burning.

   "After that we were able to work as usual. Until the descent started. At that time we noticed that weird smell again. The engine we thought was responsible for it was still shut off from providing air. So we did not have an answer for our problem.

"I was lucky – at least I thought I was – I did not feel bad in any way.

"We were flying back to Frankfurt 48 hours later. The flight was normal. We were all able to work and provide the passengers with a good service. I travelled home by train. On the way I started to feel bad and it got worse. I was able to reach home before I collapsed. I felt sick and dizzy. I felt like that for about four days. After these four days it was better and I was able to work again. I worked for about six months but realised too late that my health was getting worse. I needed more and more sleep, my energy level was very low, I had the feeling of being constantly ill and that my throat was sore all the time. In April I was not able to wake up anymore. I slept about 13-14 hours without feeling recovered at all. I felt aggressive. I got horrible headaches, felt dizzy and had no energy, was tired all the time, could not think any more, could not concentrate, I was just not able to live my daily life.

"I consulted with one doctor after the other to find out what was wrong with me. But no one could help me. My family doctor tried to get help from my employer's medical service but they just told him that they could not help at all. They didn't find any bacterial or viral infection to explain my sore throat nor did I have any allergies. I needed strong painkillers because the normal ones didn't help my headaches anymore. No one could explain why I was sleeping so much without feeling recovered. I also consulted a psychologist. I spent all my money for tests and doctors to get an explanation and a cure, but to no avail.

"More than a year later I finally found physicians who were able to tell me what the problem was. One told me that all my symptoms were a result from smelly fumes I inhaled on the plane. And he found toxins in my blood which caused all

> the symptoms and still do, and there is no antidote. I found out that there was a treatment that filters blood to cleanse it from toxins. I was able to go for two treatments. After these two treatments some symptoms got a little better and my energy level also improved. But the symptoms are still there. I still can't concentrate for long, I have a tremor and a nervous twitch in some muscles, bad headaches – often nothing helps against these headaches and sometimes they last for days – my legs hurt and feel heavy, I get tired very fast and my energy does not last long, I still need too much sleep (about 10 hours), my memory got very bad, I forget things fast and sometimes I can't even remember what I was saying two minutes ago, sometimes I want to say something but I can't find the words, my hands and feet are always cold, I can't feel cold in my fingers it just hurts, most of the time I feel like I have the flu but there is no virus or bacteria. I have been fighting for three years to get my health and my life back. My company says nothing happened. They ignore me and my symptoms." (Staying anonymous because of fear of retribution.)

I could fill a separate book with testimonies!

Toxic cabin air not only compromises the health of cabin crew and passengers, it also compromises flight safety. Pilots have described feeling groggy, or 'out of it' or even paralysed when breathing air laden with jet oil and other fumes and have been forced to don their full face oxygen masks to regain control over their faculties.

Toxic smell, fume events and residual contamination are dangerous. Period.

After completing his study with aviators, Professor Müller-Mohnssen specifically warned years ago that in years to come many, many more crewmembers would become severely sick from cabin air contamination. Unfortunately he was right. Although scientists and other experts as well as specialised groups from all over the world keep warning of the dangers, nothing has changed or is being done.

Part 3

The Non-Allopathic Way

The Change

I have only mentioned a few of the most obvious toxins floating around in which you are standing, sitting and working, day and night on longer and longer non-stop flights in an enclosed environment. There are many invisible dangers in your breathing air, to which you can be exposed on your flights that can become detrimental to your health. The only jet-aircraft to date without the bleed air problem is the Boeing 787 – but that does not exclude the presence of disinsectant spray pesticides, nor flame-retardants and other toxins.

I spoke earlier about the fact that I was advised to avoid at all cost all chemicals, including perfumes, personal hygiene products with fragrances, household cleaning products, environmental toxins and to lead a healthy stress-free life, in fresh air, with fresh clean water and organic food. NO alcohol, which I couldn't tolerate any more as it was, no smoking, which I had quit when I was 33 anyway. I had to follow a specific nutrition plan, which excluded dairy, meat, bread, coffee and tea. No meat was not a problem for me, cheese I had noticed caused me to feel unwell, and coffee I couldn't tolerate either any more.

It is essential that you follow given advice, no matter whose you choose, through to the letter without fail. I do not say that my suggestions are the one and only, not at all. But they come from my many years of experience, trial and error and after following and documenting reported improvements from others, who tried the same or similar approach.

Important: Don't start doubting and certainly don't complain after a few days that 'it's not working' or you are feeling just as bad or worse. Fact is, that when we detox one can, even will feel worse for a while, sometimes only a few days sometimes longer, depending on the grade of your toxicity and your body's ability to adapt to the detox process, and of course how you are detoxing.

It is very hard work for your body to mobilise toxins and it is imperative that we make sure they are expelled from the body.

Please note: if and when you are mobilising the toxins, you will notice it in your urine and stools, which will be very/extra smelly and also of different colours as you move along. I mention this because some people get a fright and think something is wrong. You might also smell from your mouth/breath and skin/sweat. The good news is that you know you are indeed detoxing.

This type of detox is not comparable to 'regular' detox plans you will find in magazines and on the Internet since most of them are based on weight loss regimes, or on a toxicity stemming from everyday overeating, eating wrong foods, overindulging in sweets, alcohol, smoking etc.

We are talking about detoxing a system that is fighting for survival after being harmed by toxic warfare agents that have most probably damaged the central nervous system (CNS), so extra care, patience and determination is needed.

Do not do the detox on your own, contact one of the recommended practitioners, who can help monitor changes happening, and advise when you are experiencing detox symptoms. They will also help determine the exact doses for the nutrients you will need, possibly after first testing your bloods for certain levels (e.g. vitamin D or glutathione). Each person is a complex individual and needs a different amount of micro-nutrients. Some need ten different ones, others more and again others less, or only specific ones.

Never ever try and save money by buying cheap brand micro-nutrients. It is not worth it and you could do more damage than good, and will certainly not benefit from them.

Best would be to have a physician who knows what s/he is doing as mentioned earlier, and who can give you a sick leave recommendation, in order for you to concentrate fully on your detox. In my case I was off for nine months – it does not have to be that length of time for you, that's how bad my condition was.

Do not take this lightly – if you are sure, and have the relevant diagnostics that confirm a cabin air poisoning, get down to sorting your life out and start your trip to improve your health by becoming pro-active. No excuses. No ifs or buts or shoulds, definitely no 'after the party', 'after my cousin's wedding' or 'in the New Year', or 'after the next flight' – NOW!

Mind you: don't start what you won't finish and don't stop what you have started!

If you can't follow the suggestions for whatever reason, please do contact us, or your therapist of choice who can help you overcome doubts and give you ideas what to do.

You can contact me and I can also connect you with other helpers in your country, closer to you, or affected people who have gone through the drill already. We have many kind and friendly helpers, most of them aerotoxic victims themselves, who will gladly help.

Avoid, Avoid, Avoid!

Healing is a matter of time,
but it is sometimes also a matter of opportunity.

(Hippocrates)

To begin with, avoid everything you can that could make your condition worse at all cost – this will have some major impact on most lives, so be prepared!

First and foremost avoid using, touching, ingesting, applying and inhaling chemicals – our body is NOT made to metabolise SYNTHETIC and toxic material!

This means: get rid of body and hair care products, household cleaning materials, detergents, fabric softeners, and any paints and similar products you may have put aside to use later. This may seem like a waste, but I imagine most of you have heard or read that hundreds of chemicals, including neurotoxins are in those products. So you are topping up your system with them through your skin.

Do not plan any kind of renovation in your house, no painting, wallpaper, new carpets, new wooden or plastic furniture or flooring. Do not use any pesticides, rose sprays and similar products in your houseplants or garden, or on your pets (e.g. flea collars).

Get stuck in to books and magazines that tell you all about how you can do all of this the natural way. Ladies, you can get fragrance-free make-up, hair sprays, deodorants and even organic lipsticks, mascara and cleansers.

Pay heed to where you buy clothing for yourself and your kids. Cheap clothes are usually full of formaldehyde. Also, well-known brands have been found guilty of chemical overload. Wash them 2-3 times before wearing. Black is worst!

Quit smoking: if you can't or don't want to (!), think again.

DETOX basic wisdom:

- Exposure stop
- Drink 2-2.5 litres of unpolluted water daily
- Drink herbal infusions
- Eat organic foods
- Less or no meat
- 1-2 'green' drinks daily
- Light exercise
- No smoking
- No alcohol
- No dairy products
- No sugar or other sweeteners
- Only medications you have to take
- Avoid chemicals
- Support with: see following list

Do Not Go Off Medication Without Consulting Your Physician!

Support with:

- Hot sea-salt baths
- Dry body brushing
- Infra-red light sauna
- Sauna
- Salt grotto
- Lymph-massage/massage
- Head and shoulder massage
- Reflexology
- Breuss massage (Dorn Therapy)
- Traditional Chinese medicine: Acupuncture, Tui Na
- Micronutrients
- Detox food plan

One, or better two, of these therapies per week would be advisable. If you can't go for an appointment, at least substitute with 2-3 hot sea salt baths at home.

Naturopathic Medicine works better for us.

Because the newer methods of treatment are good, it does not follow that the old ones were bad: for if our honourable and worshipful ancestors had not recovered from their ailments, you and I would not be here today.

(Confucius: 551–478 BC)

Practised for thousands of years by cultures around the world, natural medicine and health care viewed from perhaps the most famous Indian Ayurvedic or Traditional Chinese Medicine, are about detoxification, resting, cleansing and nourishing the body from the inside out. By removing and eliminating toxins, then feeding your body with healthy nutrients, detoxifying can help protect you from disease and renew your ability to maintain optimum health.

Our particular problem is though, that we are not dealing with the regular everyday accumulation of toxins or acidity from foods or beverages, smoking, alcohol and drugs consummation, but that we have to try and remove stored residue, deposited in our tissue and cells from highly toxic chemicals that we otherwise would in no way ingest voluntarily. Because they are agents found in synthetic oils used for engines, and pesticides and fungicides to kill insects.

And that is the problem.

Individualised health care draws equally from scientific evidence and the unique mind, body and spirit of the patient. Naturopathic medicine is or should be complementary to conventional medicine, and is dedicated to the study and celebration of holistic health and healing. It is committed to empowering patients to retain control over their health and wellbeing.

In our particular case we must seek to remove the toxins gently to avoid the onset of repeat symptoms – which is not always possible. In natural medicine the patient must do his or her part. It is important to continue with the detox process even if and when you have uncomfortable symptoms, it usually does mean that the toxic waste is shifting. The process is made a bit more difficult due to the fact that these neurotoxins lodge and build up in the fatty tissue, to which also the brain, the pancreas and other organs belong.

Also nowadays, the nano-technology (tiniest of tiny particles) may be causing an additional huge problem since these tiniest of particles can cross each and every natural barrier in our body. Including the blood-brain barrier!

Bear in mind that you may lose some weight, which is not the ultimate goal we are wanting to achieve, but comes along with the change of lifestyle habits – and may come as an added bonus for some. Because by losing weight we lose body fat which, by melting away, will help take a lot of toxic waste with it. The toxic waste can mimic certain symptoms and pop-up illnesses (e.g. diabetes or other endocrine abnormalities) due to the toxic overload throwing everything off balance.

I try to avoid the use of words that might sound too 'holistic', since, as you might know, there are the sceptics and doubters who will latch onto them and will try and condemn complementary medicine and the (w)holistic working practitioners to hell and back again. Although those practitioners may have degrees and studies to proof their point, or are medical physicians who have an interest in environmental medicine and in simple common sense, and who are interested in helping their patients also with unconventional methods. Many good physicians are afraid to admit using such therapies, for fear of being ridiculed by their conservative peers and colleagues, and in the past some have even been removed from the medical council registry for doing so.

What sceptics are really good at is leaving out pieces of evidence that they can't explain, and at the same time do not deliver contradictory (scientific) proof of natural medicine not working. So try not to become influenced, and make up your own mind. Personally, and I wasn't alone in this, I improved only by the use of a natural health approach: avoidance of chemicals, organic food, micro-nutrients, some therapies and change of lifestyle and if need be and can be done, change of environment. Entirely. Prescribed by Professor Müller-Mohnsson and several other highly qualified experts, scientists and physicians.

So, yes, complementary or alternative natural medicine works better for us, because of the avoidance and non-use of otherwise daily used household products and cosmetics with chemicals in them, or synthetic medication. But here's the reminder: if you are taking medication for a specific, diagnosed health issue, please do not stop taking it without consulting your medical practitioner. Get a second opinion, even a third if you do not receive answers that help you, or if you are in doubt. Doing a detox while on medication can cause an alteration of the effects of the medicine. I do not 'condemn' allopathic medicine at all, it has also helped me, and there are excellent doctors out there. It would in my opinion simply be even better if more of them would be more open-minded and complement their approach with so called alternative or natural methods.

The Power of Natural Medicine and Alternative or Complementary Therapy Treatments

Respect for the Patient.

The human body is able to restore and maintain health if one does not load it with chemicals. The western medicine physician's role should be to support the body's abilities with natural, non-toxic therapies, and to assist the patient in creating a healthy environment and lifestyle. Sadly, more often than not, they revert to medication and try to diagnose the symptoms using their list of 'approved' illnesses that have been given some fancy name with symptoms to match. Often enough it has happened that a diagnosis of e.g. 'Parkinson's Disease' or flu, or even MS has been given, or, not good at all: psychosomatic illness, which is a very stretchable and unclear diagnosis[17], instead of first 'poisoning', followed by 'Aerotoxic Injury/Syndrome'. They often diagnose without thinking 'outside-of-the-box'.

Naturopathic practitioners and physicians seek and treat the underlying cause of a disease, using therapies that are safe and effective. Symptoms are viewed as expressions of the body's natural attempt to heal, which can be hard to comprehend sometimes. Since the goal is to identify and treat the cause, naturopathic physicians avoid, and consider harmful, treatments that obscure the cause by suppressing symptoms.

The human body and mind are fully integrated aspects of a person's overall being. Each patient is a unique whole, and requires individualised and comprehensive consideration for healing to occur. With or without conventional methods, medication etc.

The naturopath's most important role is to empower the patient to reclaim command over his or her own health. The physician strives to instil the patient with hope.

Ultimately, it is the patient not the physician who achieves healing. And I have to be very clear about one thing: without you doing your part fully by following the advice given 100 percent you will, more likely than not, not achieve the result you would like. So please be prepared and willing.

You will notice that I am concentrating a lot on liver detox and support. The liver is the most important organ to detox and often is badly stressed; likely even to be damaged from the toxic onslaught.

"The liver has two mechanisms designed to convert fat-soluble chemicals into water-soluble chemicals, so that they may be easily excreted from the body via watery fluids, such as bile and urine. Phase One, to put it simply, is the pathway, which converts a toxic chemical into a less harmful chemical. But, some may be converted from relatively harmless substances into potentially carcinogenic substances.

"Excessive amounts of toxic chemicals such as pesticides can disrupt the so-called P-450 enzyme system by causing over activity. The Phase Two – detoxification pathway is called the conjugation pathway, whereby the liver cells add another substance to a toxic chemical or drug, to render it less harmful. Through conjugation, the liver is able to turn drugs, hormones and various toxins into water-soluble extractable substances. If the Phase One and Two detoxification pathways become overloaded, there will be a build-up of toxins in the body. Many of these toxins are fat-soluble and incorporate themselves into fatty parts of the body where they may stay for years, if not for a lifetime. The brain and the endocrine (hormonal) glands are fatty organs, and are common sites for fat-soluble toxins to accumulate. This may result in symptoms of brain dysfunction and hormonal imbalances, such as infertility, breast pain, menstrual disturbances, adrenal gland exhaustion and early menopause. Many of these chemicals are carcinogenic and have been implicated in the rising incidence of many cancers." (Carina Harkin BHSc)[42].

In my case, as for many others, detox Phase Two is not functioning any more. Instead of transforming and releasing the toxic waste from Phase One with the Phase Two process, the liver doesn't recognise this part anymore, and instead of releasing it sends the whole toxic waste, which by now has turned into an even more toxic cocktail, back into the system!

So the liver it is we need to concentrate on. Followed by elimination and colonic health. Of course not only, but these are very important functions of your body. The better you look after your liver and colon the more you will notice improvement in your brain function.

Let's Detox

As we grow older the indigestible residue and synthetic material accumulated through wrong food, medication, environmental toxins, electro-smog as well as alcohol, nicotine and caffeine are stored deep in our tissue instead of being expelled as is normally the case through the liver, kidneys, skin and lungs.

Toxic overload can often show with pimply skin and black spots, headaches, bloating, constipation and possibly growths. When such toxic waste is not removed our immune system becomes sluggish and dysfunctional.

A regular detox to remove harmful toxic waste left over from alcohol, nicotine, amalgam ('silver' fillings), fluoride (toothpaste), food additives and medication can be helpful. People often try some form of diet, of which there are plenty to be found on the Internet and in magazines, all praising their approach to be the best, and that they detox. Also, fasting will be one, which comes highly recommended by some to be the one and only thing to do. It is not advisable to do either, since diets tend to be 'crash diets', and fasting should only be done under supervision! Diets based on only carbohydrates or only proteins are also not advisable.

In our case of organophosphate poisoning or Aerotoxic Injury/Syndrome our immediate goal is not to lose weight, but to release toxic waste. As mentioned before you will lose some weight. But, the brain and liver are also fatty tissue, and they can't lose weight, but the toxins in them must go.

A detox involves the following basics to start with:

No sugar, no caffeine, no alcohol, no nicotine or any other form of recreational drugs.

If you are taking medication for a particular illness (blood pressure, diabetes, and so on) *PLEASE do not stop taking them without consulting your physician.*

You must also pay attention before using certain herbs that are recommended, since some may be potent medicinal herbs and could interfere with your medication.

If you are a heavy smoker, start by reducing and ease off of the nicotine within a timeframe. Set a goal. Do not use patches since you still give your body nicotine through them. And definitely do not switch to electric cigarettes. Yes, it can be done, I stopped smoking, I know!

If you are used to lots of sugar (and products with a lot of sugar) the same thing applies, ease off.

If you are a user of artificial sweeteners, PLEASE stop that ASAP, ease off the products (cokes, sodas, diabetic products) you ingest – this is one of the most toxic compounds you are putting in to your system.

If you are a drug user (this also applies for regular users of e.g. sleeping pills) or an alcoholic you must not be shy or ashamed and ask for additional professional help and support.

If you are a meat eater, please ensure you reduce your meat intake during the detox phase to three to four portions per week. Use organic lean beef or organic poultry, no pork. No cold cuts, sausages, salami and so on.

It will always be a bit more difficult for a meat eater to change their habits, but you can do it!

Reduce, better even avoid for the time being: milk, cheese, yoghurt and butter. Dairy products seem to cause mucous build-up or irritate and cause inflammation due to lactose and casein intolerance.

Introduce plenty of fresh, filtered, de-chlorinated water and unsweetened herbal teas (a total minimum required is around 2-2.5 litres per day).

One to two glasses of fresh water with some fresh lemon juice upon awakening, followed by two cups of stinging nettle or dandelion tea in the mornings will already do a lot for you.

Start slowly by adding bitter foods, i.e. salads with chicory, endives, radicchio, frisée and rocket, as well as gently steamed vegetables (broccoli, sprouts). For your sweet tooth, eat fruit.

Then continue after about one week of adjustment, which you may notice through some bloating, or diarrhoea, or headaches, with the introduction of foods, herbs and fruit I have listed as examples in the following. You will find plenty of cookbooks if you need help with their preparation, or for ideas. For a personalised detox, nutrition and supplementation plan you can also contact me.

One more thing before you start: you might have setbacks; setbacks are only ever devastating when one thinks they'll last forever. Small or even big setbacks in how you feel are possible, to be expected and normal.

Introduce the New

Introduce the new into your life and welcome it with an open mind, no matter how miserable you may feel. Bear in mind that it is being done to help improve your health and subsequently your quality of life. Do not ever say you can't do it – if you do, you won't!

Treatments and therapies are excellent to support the detox process, especially when chosen carefully for that purpose. I am introducing a few of those I have tried myself and have found very beneficial.

Ayurveda and Traditional Chinese Medicine[43, 44]

In Ayurveda a person is viewed as a unique individual made up of five primary elements. The elements are ether (space), air, fire, water and earth. Just as in nature, we too have these five elements within us. When any of these elements are present in the environment, they will in turn have an influence on us. The foods we eat and the weather are just two examples of the presence of these elements. While we are a composite of these five primary elements, certain elements are seen to have an ability to combine to create various physiological functions.

Panchakarma

Panchakarma is a lengthy treatment offered wherever you find an Ayurveda centre worldwide. It can be quite 'heavy' on the system especially if you are not used to detox, but it is highly effective and I do not know anyone who didn't say afterwards how much better they felt and that the effect lasted up to six or more months. The added benefit here is that you are supervised during the various steps and administrations, which is a good thing and there is or should be always an Ayurvedic physician available.

Panchakarma includes the removal of toxins accumulated in the entire body and involves the use of herbal infusions in and through all orifices.

Oil Pulling

Oil pulling is a technique that involves swishing a tablespoon of sunflower seed oil in your mouth for about 5-8 minutes. This action draws out toxins in your body, primarily to improve oral health. It removes bacteria, strengthens your gums, and helps whiten teeth a little. After spitting it out, carefully scrape your tongue clean and thoroughly brush your teeth as usual (use aloe vera or other herbal toothpaste or baking soda if possible).

For the sceptics: an Ayurvedic doctor studies five and a half years including a one-year internship. The curriculum includes studying and teaching of modern anatomy, physiology, principles of medicine, preventive and social medicine, pharmacology, toxicology, forensic medicine, ENT, ophthalmology, principles of surgery, etc., along with Ayurveda topics.

Traditional Chinese Medicine – TCM

The *Yellow Emperor's Inner Canon*, the oldest received work of Chinese medical theory, was compiled around the first century BCE on the basis of shorter texts from different medical lineages. Written in the form of dialogues between the legendary Yellow Emperor and his ministers, it offers explanations on the relation between humans, their environment, and the cosmos, on the contents of the body, on human vitality and pathology, on the symptoms of illness, and on how to make diagnostic and therapeutic decisions in light of all these factors.

Traditional Chinese Medicine is a broad range of medical practices sharing common concepts including various forms of herbal medicine, acupuncture, massage, exercise and dietary therapy. It is primarily used as a complementary or alternative medicine approach.

TCM gives detailed prescriptions of these patterns regarding their typical symptoms, mostly including characteristic tongue and/or pulse findings. An example:

'Up Flaming Liver Fire':

Headaches, red face, reddened eyes, dry mouth, nosebleeds, dry or hard stools, profuse menstruation, sudden tinnitus or deafness, vomiting of sour or bitter fluids, expectoration of blood, irascibility, impatience, aggressiveness, red tongue with dry yellow fur, slippery and string-like pulse.

This description is very close to what an aerotoxic victim's liver points feel like, and symptoms we as poisoned people have.

For the sceptics: the Doctor of Traditional Chinese Medicine is a ten-semester study programme that deeply explores areas of medicine such as psychology, oncology, gerontology, acupuncture, detox, research and the classic texts that first recorded the principles of this powerful and ancient system of medicine.

Please ensure that your TCM, Ayurvedic or herbal practitioner is fully qualified and licenced to practise. Herbs are potent natural healers and must be prescribed, blended and administered carefully and the manual therapies must be given skilfully.

Tui Na Massage

Tui Na Massage is based on a full TCM case history using the four examinations to identify a complaint, an underlying pattern and treatment principles. Techniques are at the heart of any system of bodywork. They are what define its feel and therapeutic qualities. Most textbooks on Chinese massage list between thirty and seventy 'shoe fa' (hand techniques). The massage therapist can apply hand techniques to particular areas, channels, or acupressure points, achieving similar results to acupuncture needles.

Equally important is the way the techniques are carried out. The Chinese practitioner says that the hand technique must be gentle and soft, yet deep and penetrating. The strokes must be applied rhythmically and persistently. The controlled use of very deep, moving pressure is one of the secrets of Tui Na massage.

I have experienced huge benefits from this type of massage. The very deep controlled pressure technique 'on the spot' is amazing! The best treatment I received was from a blind Chinese therapist who later on taught me the technique.

Acupuncture[45, 46]

Acupuncture is a therapy most have heard about. It is about the stimulation of specific acupuncture points along the so-called meridians along the body using very thin needles.

Acupuncture is particularly effective for pain relief, nausea and vomiting after surgery or chemotherapy. Both the World Health Organisation (WHO) and the National Institute of Health recognise that acupuncture can be a helpful part of a treatment plan for many illnesses. A partial list includes: addiction (such as alcoholism), asthma, bronchitis, carpal tunnel syndrome, constipation, diarrhoea, facial tics, fibromyalgia, headaches, irregular menstrual cycles, poly-cystic ovarian syndrome, lower back pain, menopausal symptoms, menstrual cramps, osteoarthritis, sinusitis and spastic colon (often called IBS or irritable bowel syndrome). You can safely combine acupuncture with prescription drugs and other conventional treatments.

Massage, Lymph-massage

Massage is generally considered part of complementary and alternative medicine. It's increasingly being offered along with standard treatment for a wide range of medical conditions and situations. Studies of the benefits of massage demonstrate that it is an effective treatment for reducing stress, pain and muscle tension. Studies have found massage may also be helpful for:

- Digestive disorders
- Fibromyalgia
- Headaches
- Insomnia related to stress
- Lymphatic blockages

I regularly availed of full body massages, just to help remove tension and of course activate the circulation flow to remove toxins from the tissue.

Reflexology[47]

Reflexology is a manual therapy focusing on the soles of the feet by applying pressure with the thumbs and fingers on certain points to stimulate organs, nerve endings and energy pathways to promote health. History has it that similar techniques are recorded in China and Egypt, but one will also find that in Ayurveda the feet are treated with pressure techniques.

Though reflexology works on different principles to Western medicine, and there is little 'scientific' evidence to back up its effectiveness, my clients, and hundreds of thousands of others worldwide, insist that their general health and wellbeing improved. I think that is evidence enough. The belief is that reflexology stimulates the body into healing itself by improving circulation, reducing stress, pain and restoring natural balance.

When our body's defences break down due to stressors, like chemicals entering our system, we become more susceptible to illness and disease. Reflexology reduces general stress levels by activating deep tranquil relaxation, helping the body to balance itself and allowing the energy to flow more freely.

Our blood needs to flow freely throughout the body to carry oxygen and nutrients to all the cells and by removing the waste products of toxins. By reducing stress and tension, reflexology allows the cardiovascular system to flow more naturally and easily.

Reflexology also stimulates the lymphatic system. It cleanses the body of toxins and impurities and also stimulates the production of endorphins, leading to an improved immune system and sense of wellbeing.

After my first reflexology session I was hooked – the experience of pure relaxation (I always fell asleep a few minutes into the treatment and afterwards walked away goggle-eyed, I was so relaxed) is a huge benefit for your body system; that alone, if nothing else, helps tremendously to release toxic waste.

Biofeedback[48]

When you raise your hand to wave to a friend, or lift your foot to take another step up the stairs, you control these actions. Other body functions like heart rate, skin temperature and blood pressure are controlled involuntarily by your nervous system. You don't think about making your heart beat faster or to breathe. It just happens.

One technique can help you gain more control over these normally involuntary functions. It's called biofeedback, and the therapy is used to help prevent or treat conditions, including migraine headaches, chronic pain, incontinence and high blood pressure.

The idea behind biofeedback is that by harnessing the power of your mind and becoming aware of what's going on inside your body, you can gain more control over your health.

Chronic pain. By helping you identify tight muscles and then learn to relax those muscles, biofeedback may help relieve the discomfort of conditions like lower back pain, abdominal pain, temporomandibular joint disorders (TMJ) and fibromyalgia.

Headaches. Headaches are one of the best-studied biofeedback uses. Muscle tension and stress can trigger migraines and other types of headaches, and can make headache symptoms worse. There is good evidence that biofeedback therapy can relax muscles and ease stress to reduce both the frequency and severity of headaches. Biofeedback seems to be especially beneficial for headaches.

Anxiety. Anxiety relief is one of the most common uses of biofeedback. Biofeedback lets you become more aware of your body's responses when you're stressed and anxious. Then you can learn how to control those responses.

Therapeutic Apheresis

Quite a few aerotoxic victims have availed of 'therapeutic apheresis', and where some immediately reported huge improvement in how they felt, others had to have several treatments before noticing a longer lasting effect. But this could depend on the severity of toxic load. However, according to some doctors with whom I personally agree, the toxins don't just accumulate in the plasma (plasma = extra cellular fluid, which is the only part cleaned by the apheresis machine), they also accumulate inside our body's cells and tissue where they block all sorts of normal cell function which is not cleaned by apheresis. I have spoken about the storage in fatty tissue previously. To regain health, those intracellular toxins have to go.

Plasmapheresis: Within the plasma are contained antibodies and antigen-antibody complexes that may contribute to the deleterious effects of autoimmune diseases. Removal of the plasma (and replacement with saline solution) will help to reduce circulating antibodies and immune complexes. In rare circumstances excess blood proteins are present that may cause circulatory problems.

You may know the other type of this filtration-cleansing technique called dialysis, which cleanses e.g. a person's non-functioning kidneys. The difference is in the filters used and the amount of times the procedure is repeated, plus of course the evaluation of the exchanged fluid.

I have, on several occasions of toxic symptoms episodes that happened due to some unexpected exposure, had 2-3 saline solution drips administered, plus some pure oxygen, and added glutathione, which helped me a lot. I have not done the apheresis myself.

Liver/Gallstone Cleanse

Although the liver cleanse is an age-old practice, the modern liver cleanse has been widely promoted and made known once again worldwide mainly by Dr Hulda Clark (www.drclarke.net). The bile duct system is a gigantic tree with lots of interconnecting branches. There are miles of bile ducts in the liver. The liver cleanses itself by making bile and sends its toxins with the bile into the intestine. It is made of water, cholesterol, bile acids and its salts, proteins, bilirubin and fatty acids. It is produced by the liver cells and is stored in the gallbladder. Dr Clarke did not invent this cleanse (to my knowledge) particularly for a detox of chemicals/poisons, but as a general health cleanse. But, taking from the list of benefits just a few, improved lymphatic function and removal of mycotoxins from the liver, allowing it to function better – there's nothing wrong with that! Once again I am reminded of 'star wars' between the allopathic world, who tend to rip it apart and ridicule it, and on the other hand those who have actually benefited from doing this liver cleanse. Many clients of mine tried it and all reported back with positive results.

Colon Cleansing Methods

The body naturally produces wastes from its own biological processes. In addition, as we now know, we are exposed to a multitude of deadly elements.

If my experience is any indication, and should you hopefully decide to do something for your body, you stand at the threshold of an amazing experience of wellbeing.

The colon walls are not made of rock and have a downside, they are not leak proof. They can absorb toxins from the faeces. These toxins then travel into the blood circulation. Since the liver filters all the blood, toxins absorbed into the bloodstream through colon walls put a strain on the liver. Can you see why colon cleansing is so important?

Earlier on I mentioned the Panchakarma colonic cleanses, here are a few more:

Fasting, for example, which is not appropriate for everyone, yet can be one of the best colon cleansing methods for some. But please, fasting must be done under supervision! Hydro Therapy is also good, but not enough. The Coffee Enema by the Gerson Method, which I used in the beginning upon recommendation of one of my physicians, can be done at home if you don't want to go for hydro/colonic therapy, which can be a bit intimidating and embarrassing. Herbal detoxification also has pros and cons everyone should know about, but is in the meantime my favourite, and has many more pros than cons. Even lots of dietary fibre or bulk colon cleanse products may or may not be right for you.

You could also choose a herbal concoction called 'Essiac' which you can make yourself like I did, or just freshly juiced wheat grass, once or twice per day. I found the best method for me was a twice per year twenty-one-day detox with herbs and herbal tinctures[49], and in between those a daily double dose of fresh wheat grass, which gave me a lot of my energy back!

It is important not to use over-the-counter products that cause diarrhoea; these do not cleanse the bowels properly.

You will of course notice some difference in bowel movements after changing your food plan to more of what I have recommended. Especially if you start taking a green juice/smoothie with wheat grass first thing in the morning. But that is not quite enough since a lot of (really yucky) mucous plaque is stuck to the colon walls loaded with toxic waste, causing inflammation; this needs to be removed. Some additional help can only achieve this through one of the above-mentioned herbal methods. Personally I do feel most comfortable and have been most successful with methods working from the inside out, starting in the mouth.

Good Gut Bacteria

Probiotics are live bacteria and yeasts that are good for your health, especially your digestive system. We usually think of bacteria as something that causes diseases. But your body is full of bacteria, both good and bad. Probiotics are often called good or helpful bacteria because they help keep your gut healthy.

Probiotics are naturally found in your body. You can also find them in some foods and supplements. Traditional diets around the world have typically included raw and fermented foods teeming with bacteria, including many beneficial strains. From yoghurt to kefir, to sauerkraut to fermented fish, cultures around the world include good gut bacteria in their diet. You will notice a difference in how your bowels work and how you feel if the bacteria balance is healthy. I took, along with the herbal cleanse, daily portions of good bacteria. If you are a person who has constipation problems, adding probiotics to your diet on a regular, even daily, basis can be helpful.

Dorn Treatment

You may find that you also have back issues, tight muscles, sciatic nerve pain, frozen shoulders, stiff neck and so on. The Dorn therapy is a non-invasive, gentle yet very effective treatment, which will help alleviate those problems by freeing up and loosening those stiff areas. I prefer it to chiropractic sessions which I find too rough and require many more treatments. The gentle Dorn and Breuss treatment releases tension and allows tissue to release toxins, especially the Breuss spinal massage. You must try that, it is wonderful and effective!

In Dorn therapy, meridian lines are referred to, which are connecting lines between the acupuncture points. Energy flow can be inhibited by tension or strengthened by treatment and can work backwards or forwards. Also, medical professionals use the Dorn method in their practice. It is very successful and a widely known treatment not only in German-speaking parts of Europe but also elsewhere. It is well accepted; some health insurers even pay for this treatment.

Other Excellent Treatments without a Therapist's Involvement

Sauna

Although I personally prefer the infra-red light sauna to the regular sauna, some might enjoy the hotter sauna more. Just be aware that a prolonged stay in a sauna may lead to the loss of electrolytes from the body. Regular sipping of water or fruit juices during the sauna reduces the risk of dehydration. Sauna has been recommended for reducing symptoms in chronic fatigue syndrome, fibromyalgia and rheumatoid arthritis. The sauna releases lots of toxic waste through the skin by sweating. You can aid that, especially if you are a poor sweater, by dry brushing your skin. Please try not to wear a bathing suit, if you want to cover yourself use a bath towel. One to two sessions per week are advisable.

Far Infra-Red Sauna

Infra-red rays are waves of energy, which are totally invisible to the naked eye and are capable of penetrating deep into the human body, where they gently raise the body's temperature and activate major bodily functions. Some recent experimental and clinical scientific studies from Japan have shown that far infra-red therapy results in more rapid wound healing that was independent of changes in blood flow and skin temperature. Far infra-red therapy helped this healing by stimulating a group of cells called fibroblasts to make more collagen, which is a very important part of good wound healing and tissue building. The gentle tissue warming has also been shown to help improve the 'health' of the cells, which if left untreated may increase the risk of other health disorders. One to three sessions per week.

The Salt Grotto

That salt caves were healthy, a Polish physician discovered as far back as 1843. Men working in salt mines were a lot less sick or did not suffer from respiratory issues compared to coal miners or the general population. The microclimate, which is produced within the salt caves, is very effective for the cleansing of the respiratory system, the blood and whole body; they are great for your everyday health, relaxation and wellbeing. These sessions where you are surrounded by rock or even Himalayan crystal salt will help:

- Ease stress;
- Reduce joint and inflammation pain;
- Ease insomnia;
- Assist your muscles to recover from physical exhaustion and fatigue;
- Strengthen your immune system;
- Clear your head.

These sessions mimic the wonderful healing effects of the natural salt caves and other salt rich environments. All places where the negative ions in the air help to rebalance your physical and energetic systems are good for you. In addition to the restorative benefits of these sessions they provide therapeutic benefits that can also support and revive your respiratory and other pulmonary health issues, such as:

- Chronic ear/nose/throat ailments;
- Asthma;
- Bronchitis and sinusitis;
- Allergy symptoms;
- Emphysema and COPD;

- Cold and stuffy head;
- Skin ailments: acne, eczema, psoriasis and dermatitis.

As you can see, many of the symptoms an aerotoxic victim has are covered, and I can confirm that it really does help. After experiencing the fantastic effects myself I built a small salt grotto room in my health farm, which was very busy being used not only by myself but also by people coming for help with respiratory and skin issues.

Exercises

Most aerotoxic victims are stressed out, some become anxious and are afraid of what might happen with them. Most cannot sleep properly anymore and become over tired and restless. For this I recommend one or the other of the following exercises. They are gentle and will not cause additional stress on your system.

Yoga

I will only mention a few of the many wonderful benefits that yoga offers, which in my opinion are most helpful.

Most of us take shallow breaths and don't give much thought to how we breathe. Yoga breathing exercises focus on the breath and teach us how to take deeper ones, which benefits the entire body. Certain types of yoga breathing can also help clear the nasal passages and help calm the central nervous system.

Concentrating intently on what your body is doing has the effect of bringing calmness to the mind. And of course stress reduction. Physical activity is good for relieving stress, and this is particularly true of yoga.

If you don't feel like doing yoga you should consider doing at least breathing exercises. Proper breathing is hugely beneficial. Take up singing, it teaches you how to breathe properly! I would love to sing, but my dogs get very worried when I do...

By making a conscious decision to focus on our breath for a

part of each day, we can make it so that we regularly breathe deeper without having to think about it at all. Post sticky notes around your home as reminders; when you see them, breathe deeply. Breathing deeply for just a few minutes every day will improve your mental outlook and physical health.

Meditation

I began meditation practices when I was sixteen. Although I haven't been consistent I do use meditation a lot. Sometimes it is just about sitting in nature under a tree or lying on the grass allowing your thoughts to travel into the dream world of your imagination. The term daydreaming can also refer to a form of meditation, as long as you do not think about your shopping list and chores to do! Add breathing exercises to your daydream and some 'progressive muscle relaxation' (PMR) and you will relax. This is essential to help detox.

Progressive muscle relaxation is a technique that involves tensing specific muscle groups, then relaxing them to create awareness of tension and relaxation. It is termed progressive because it proceeds through all major muscle groups, relaxing them one at a time, and eventually leads to total muscle relaxation.

Meditation has been linked to larger amounts of grey matter in the hippocampus and frontal areas of the brain. More grey matter can lead to more positive emotions, longer-lasting emotional stability, and heightened focus during daily life. Meditation has also been shown to diminish age-related effects on grey matter and reduce the decline of our cognitive functioning, which is another part of our problems.

One of the things meditation has been linked to is improving rapid memory recall.

Positive Thinking

In general I am a positive, optimistic person and also have the gift of being able to motivate others. Still, once in while during the worst phases of horrible symptoms from the aerotoxic poisoning, sometimes it went downhill and I also used some methods to reactivate my positive thinking abilities. It always worked.

Some studies show that personality traits like optimism and pessimism can affect many areas of your health and wellbeing. The positive thinking that typically comes with optimism is a key part of effective stress management. And effective stress management is associated with many health benefits. If you tend to be pessimistic, don't despair – you can learn positive thinking skills. Positive thinking doesn't mean that you keep your head in the sand and ignore life's less pleasant situations. Positive thinking just means that you approach unpleasantness in a more positive and productive way. You think the best is going to happen, not the worst. Positive thinking can even start with self-talk, which is the endless stream of unspoken thoughts that run through your head. These automatic thoughts can be positive or negative. Catch yourself with negative thoughts or just single words even, and change them into positive ones.

Nordic Walking

I took up Nordic walking because of all the additional benefits compared to regular walking and because the sticks helped me over the time period when I was too weak and wobbly without them and needed the support; the other benefit is that the whole body is moving using them.

Nordic walking exerts beneficial effects on the resting heart rate, blood pressure, exercise capacity, maximal oxygen consumption and quality of life in people with various diseases and can thus be recommended to a wide range of people as primary and secondary prevention.

Recent studies by the Cooper Institute, Dallas, showed that Nordic walking burned more calories, increased oxygen consumption, and can be up to 46 percent more efficient than normal walking. The increase of oxygen is the most important factor in my opinion; it helps 'clean' and re-freshen the cells.

Enjoy as much fresh air as possible and, if you can, walk in forests, or up mountains where the air is full of goodness. Go for a walk after a thunderstorm and in the rain.

There is a tangible freshness and a specific smell of the outdoors following the drama of a big thunderstorm. Apart from the ozone and the pleasant petrichor scent that has been created when the rain hits the ground. Some plants secrete oils during dry periods, and when it rains, these oils are released into the air.

So take deep breathes!

Part 4

Fresh Food for Cell Energy

Orthomolecular Medicine

One of the most important parts of finding your way back to health, energy and wellbeing is by taking certain, very much needed, supplements, so called micro-nutrients. When I say 'very much needed', it applies to aerotoxic victims. In practically all cases nutrients have been depleted from the toxicity in the cells, nerves and tissue and need to be refilled.

Professor Müller-Mohnson gave me a very high dose which helped, and which I missed when I didn't take them. Fifteen years later when I got the acute second dose of contaminated cabin air, I needed supplementation again, this time a different combination. In the meantime the quality of such products had improved drastically, so had the prices for top quality, but please do not make the wrong decision, do not buy cheap supermarket brands.

"It is the preservation of good health and the treatment of disease by varying the concentrations in the human body of substances that are normally present in the body." [sometimes adding: "and are required for health"] (Freeman, New York, 1986)[50]

Orthomolecules are primary in medical diagnosis and treatment. The safe and effective use of nutrients, enzymes, hormones and other naturally occurring molecules is essential to assure a reasonable standard of care in medical practice.

Founded on the science of molecular biochemistry, orthomolecular medicine establishes that genetic factors affect not only the physical characteristics of individuals, but also their biochemical environment. Orthomolecular medicine, as conceptualised by double Nobel laureate Linus Pauling, aims to restore the optimum environment of the body by correcting molecular imbalances on the basis of individual biochemistry. Linus Pauling first used the term orthomolecular meaning 'correct molecule', in 1968. (www.orthomolecular.org) [50, 51]

Vitamins, Minerals, Enzymes, Amino Acids

The following list of choice micro-nutrients is to help replenish the ones that have been used up or are needed in a higher quantity due to the effects of Aerotoxic Syndrome, and to help regain your health by strengthening the immune system. The descriptions are kept short, but can be looked up for further in-depth information, as listed in the reference list (see Maryland University)[52]. We have discovered that specific combinations and amounts (dosage) are vital for each individual, so please make sure to discuss this with one of our experts or a professional of your choice, who is well versed in orthomolecular medicine and toxicology.

Most of them have benefits which help improve, or get rid of symptoms you may be experiencing, and are very helpful when taken regularly, since, due to the lack of them the above mentioned symptoms as are experienced with Aerotoxic Injury/Syndrome are likely to stay, or worse even increase.

In the fight against the poisoning your body will have used up most, if not all, resources and micro-nutrients stored in its cells, so replacement is essential!

B1-Thiamine

Thiamine is found in both plants and animals and plays a crucial role in certain metabolic reactions. Your body needs it to form adenosine triphosphate (ATP), which every cell of the body uses for energy. Symptoms of thiamine deficiency are fatigue, irritability, depression and abdominal discomfort. People with thiamine deficiency also have trouble digesting carbohydrates. Good dietary sources of thiamine include whole grain or enriched cereals and rice, legumes, wheat germ, bran, brewer's yeast and blackstrap molasses. For several months I drank 1 cup of hot water with blackstrap molasses; it tasted horrible at first, but I got used to it. It's a cheap and healthy B1 source.

B2-Riboflavin

In addition to producing energy for the body, riboflavin also works as an antioxidant by fighting damaging particles in the body known as free radicals. Free radicals can damage cells and DNA. Several studies suggest that people who get migraines may reduce how often they get migraines and how long they last by taking riboflavin. The best sources of riboflavin include brewer's yeast, almonds, organ meats, whole grains, wheat germ, wild rice, mushrooms, soybeans (milk), yoghurt, eggs, broccoli, Brussels sprouts and spinach. Flours and cereals are often fortified with riboflavin. I eat a lot of Brussels sprouts and broccoli, in fact daily, also organic yoghurt and eggs. Careful with milk, which I do not recommend due to the mucous producing effect it can have, which clogs up the system, or you might be lactose intolerant without knowing it. But you can get lactose-free dairy products these days. See how you manage without them and notice the difference.

B3-Niacin

Symptoms of mild deficiency include indigestion, fatigue, canker sores, vomiting, depression and Alzheimer's disease. Population studies show that people who get higher levels of niacin in their diet have a lower risk of Alzheimer's disease. B3 is found in beets, brewer's yeast, beef liver, beef kidney, fish, salmon, swordfish, tuna, sunflower seeds and peanuts. Bread and cereals are usually fortified with niacin. In addition, foods that contain tryptophan, an amino acid the body converts into niacin, include poultry, red meat, eggs and dairy products. Do not take unless prescribed by your medical or naturopathic health care practitioner.

B6-Pyridoxine

Symptoms of serious deficiency include muscle weakness, nervousness, irritability, depression, difficulty concentrating and short-term memory loss. Good food sources of vitamin B6 include chicken, turkey, tuna, salmon, shrimp, beef liver, milk, cheese, lentils, beans, spinach, carrots, brown rice, bran, sunflower seeds, wheat germ and whole grain flour. Definitely all those mentioned symptoms are noticeable when one is poisoned!

B12

If you find that you are always tired or you actually suffer from chronic fatigue, there's a good chance that you're not getting enough vitamin B12 in your diet. Vitamin B12 helps provide your body with energy. Try using it if you always feel sluggish and/or tired. Adding more vitamin B12 to your diet is good for your health, but it's also good for your brain. Studies have shown that vitamin B12 can actually improve your mental capacity and help you to stay stable emotionally. As a vegetarian, although ova-lacto, I like adding B12 once in a while.

Coenzyme Q10

CoQ10 is a substance that's found naturally in the body and helps convert food into energy. CoQ10 is found in almost every cell in the body, and it is a powerful antioxidant. Antioxidants fight damaging particles in the body known as free radicals, which damage cell membranes, tamper with DNA and even cause cell death. Scientists believe free radicals contribute to the ageing process, as well as a number of health problems, including heart disease and cancer. Antioxidants, such as CoQ10, can neutralise free radicals[53] and may reduce or even help prevent some of the damage they cause. Primary dietary sources of CoQ10 include oily fish, such as salmon and tuna – careful where they come from, they can be contaminated! Organ meats (such as liver from grass fed animals only, if at all) and whole grains (organic) are also good sources. Most people get enough CoQ10 through a balanced diet, but supplements may help people with particular health conditions. For a long time I took 250mg of coQ10 (Ubiquinol) daily, which was a great help; without it I had no energy.

Magnesium

Every organ in the body, especially the heart, muscles and kidneys needs the mineral magnesium. It also contributes to the make-up of teeth and bones. Most important, it activates enzymes, contributes to energy production and helps regulate calcium levels, as well as copper, zinc, potassium, vitamin D and other important nutrients in the body. Symptoms of magnesium deficiency may include agitation and anxiety, restless leg syndrome (RLS), sleep disorders, irritability, nausea and vomiting, abnormal heart rhythms, low blood pressure, confusion, muscle spasm and weakness, hyperventilation, insomnia, poor nail growth and even seizures.

A few studies suggest that taking magnesium supplements could help prevent migraine headaches. Sources of magnesium include, for instance, tofu, legumes, whole grains, green leafy vegetables, wheat bran, Brazil nuts, soybean flour, almonds, cashews, blackstrap molasses, pumpkin and squash seeds, pine nuts and black walnuts. Also, peanuts, oats, beet, spinach, pistachio nuts, oatmeal, bananas, baked potatoes, chocolate (dark or black chocolate only) and cocoa powder. Many herbs, spices and seaweeds supply magnesium, such as seaweed, coriander, dill, celery seed, sage, dried mustard, basil, cocoa powder, fennel seed, savory, cumin seed, tarragon, marjoram and poppy seed.

Selenium

Selenium is an essential mineral found in small amounts in the body. It works as an antioxidant, especially when combined with vitamin E. Antioxidants like selenium help fight damaging particles in the body known as free radicals. Selenium plays a role in thyroid function and many studies suggest that the body needs selenium in order for the immune system to work properly. Selenium, along with other minerals, can help build up white blood cells, which boosts the body's ability to fight illness and infection. Brewer's yeast and wheat germ, liver, butter, fish (mackerel, tuna, halibut, flounder, herring, smelts) and shellfish (oysters, scallops and lobster), garlic, whole grains, sunflower seeds and Brazil nuts (4-5 daily suffice) are all good sources of selenium.

Zinc

Zinc is an essential trace mineral, so you get it through the foods you eat. Next to iron, zinc is the most common mineral in the body and is found in every cell. It has been used since ancient times to help heal wounds and plays an important role in the immune system, reproduction, growth, taste, vision and smell, blood clotting, and proper insulin and thyroid function. Zinc also has antioxidant properties, meaning it helps protect cells in the body from damage caused by free radicals. Best sources of zinc are oysters (richest source, but careful where they come from), red meats, poultry, cheese (Ricotta, Swiss, Dutch Gouda), shrimp, crab and other shellfish – again, be careful where they come from as I'm afraid they are prone to being contaminated! Other good, though less easily absorbed, sources of zinc include legumes (especially lima beans, black-eyed peas, pinto beans, soybeans, peanuts), whole grains, miso, tofu, brewer's yeast, cooked greens, mushrooms, green beans, tahini, and pumpkin and sunflower seeds.

Gingko

Ginkgo has a long history of being used in traditional medicine to treat blood disorders and improve memory, and it's best known today as a way to potentially keep your memory sharp. There is some scientific evidence to back that up. At first, doctors thought it helped because it improves blood flow to the brain. Now more studies suggest it may protect nerve cells that are damaged in Alzheimer's disease. A number of studies have found that ginkgo has a positive effect on memory and thinking in people with Alzheimer's or vascular dementia. I have used ginkgo as a great helper during my worst brain-fog days, and find it very effective.

Ginseng

Ginseng has been used in Chinese medicine for thousands of years. The name 'ginseng' refers to both American and Asian or Korean ginsengs, which are made up of similar chemicals. Siberian ginseng, on the other hand, is a completely different plant and does not have the same active ingredients. Asian ginseng seems to be an antioxidant. Antioxidants help rid the body of free radicals, substances that can damage DNA. People who take ginseng often say they feel more alert. Several studies report that Asian ginseng may slightly improve thinking or learning. Asian ginseng is sometimes called an 'adaptogen', something that helps the body deal with physical or mental stress.

Glutathione

Glutathione-S-transferase is the most powerful internal antioxidant and liver protector. It can be depleted by large amounts of toxins and/or drugs passing through the liver, as well as starvation or fasting. It has been widely researched and is validated by over twice the number of scientific articles than vitamin C has. Nutritional authorities have stated that they believe glutathione to be as indispensable to the maintenance of our system as food, water and oxygen. Mitochondria provide energy to the cells throughout the body, without them our cells would die and we would quickly deteriorate and age. Glutathione detoxifies your blood and battles the free radicals that attack your mitochondria, saving your body from oxidative stress. Glutathione plays a vital role in protecting the body from premature aging as well as diabetes.

There are a few vegetables that are higher-grade glutathione boosters. These include asparagus, avocados, broccoli, spinach and tomatoes. Cruciferous vegetables in the mustard family, such as Brussels sprouts, cabbage, cauliflower and kale, have also been noted to be super foods for glutathione production. Fresh meats and eggs are also bursting with crucial amino acids. Non-denatured whey protein has been mentioned as useful in the quest for a higher level of glutathione.

Omega-3

Omega-3 fatty acids are considered essential fatty acids: they are necessary for human health, but since the body can't make them you have to get them through food. Omega-3 fatty acids can be found in fish, such as salmon, tuna and halibut, as well as in other sea foods including algae and krill, some plants, and nut oils. Also known as polyunsaturated fatty acids, omega-3 fatty acids play a crucial role in brain function, as well as normal growth and development. Omega-3 fatty acids are highly concentrated in the brain and appear to be important for cognitive (brain memory and performance) and behavioural function. Another difference between fish oil and krill oil is that krill oil also contains the antioxidant astaxanthin. Research shows that, due to astaxanthin's potent antioxidant activity, it may be beneficial in cardiovascular, immune, inflammatory and neurodegenerative diseases. Some research supports the assumption that it may protect body tissues from oxidative and ultraviolet damage – you can find excellent information on Dr Mercola's website under 'articles'. I by far prefer krill oil due to the cleaner environment where it is harvested and its higher potency in omega-3. Some studies have shown that krill oil may be 48 times more potent than fish oil. Two different studies have shown that taking 800 to 900mg of DHA per day for sixteen to twenty-four weeks resulted in significant improvements in memory, verbal fluency scores and rate of learning. An experiment, which I conducted on myself, by taking 3x2 capsules a day, gave me a marked improvement of brain function. (See also further along 'coconut oil'.)

Vitamin C

Our bodies are not able to produce vitamin C nor can they store it. It is essential that you eat plenty of fruit and vegetables that have a high source of the C-vitamins. Mangoes, papayas, pineapple and berries to mention a few, and broccoli, all colours of peppers, tomatoes – but remember, wash them well and try to buy organic produce.

Vitamin E

Vitamin E is a fat-soluble vitamin found in many foods, fats and oils. It is also an antioxidant. Symptoms of serious vitamin E deficiency include muscle weakness, loss of muscle mass, abnormal eye movements, vision problems and unsteady walking. The richest source of vitamin E is wheat germ. Other foods that contain a significant amount of vitamin E include liver, eggs, almonds and walnuts, sunflower seeds, cold-pressed vegetable oils, including olive, safflower, canola, dark green leafy vegetables like spinach and kale, beet, collard, mustard, turnip, sweet potatoes, avocado, asparagus and yams.

Vitamin D3

Vitamin D is also involved in regulating the immune system and cells. Getting the proper amount of vitamin D may help prevent several serious health conditions. There are two dietary forms of vitamin D: cholecalciferol and ergocalciferol. These are naturally found in foods and are added to milk. Not all yoghurt and cheese are fortified with vitamin D.

Food sources of vitamin D include cod liver oil (best source). Cod liver oil often contains very high levels of vitamin A, which can be toxic over time. Ask your health care provider about this source of vitamin D. Fatty fish such as salmon, mackerel, sardines and herring, vitamin D-fortified milk and cereal, and eggs (organic only) are also useful sources.

Your body makes vitamin D when your skin is exposed to the sun.

But remember that suntan lotions also have plenty of chemicals in them, so personally I don't use those any more. Just don't get burned by staying too long in the sun and avoid the midday sun!

And by the way: If you think you are safe because of the term 'hypo-allergenic' (and this applies to all your cosmetic products etc.), don't! The term means 'below normal' or 'slightly' allergenic. It is used to describe items that cause or are claimed to cause fewer allergic reactions. The term lacks a medical definition.

Regarding SPF factor: Some sunscreen chemicals can penetrate the skin and potentially cause more cell damage than they prevent. When exposed to UV radiation, some sunscreen ingredients generate reactive oxygen species, a class of free radicals that can damage DNA throughout the body. Reduced exposure to ultraviolet light in sunlight can contribute to vitamin D deficiency.

L-Tyrosine

Tyrosine is one of the most important amino acids, which is used in the synthesis of structural proteins. Although proteins are made up of different other amino acids, tyrosine is considered to be the most important one, because it is used in the production of neurotransmitters. Some researchers say that tyrosine directly affects the brain. Tyrosine is involved in so many vital functions that it is considered to be an all-purpose amino acid. The body tries to manage and balance the level of tyrosine, depending on the life circumstances of the individual. A high level of stress on a daily basis may result in the depletion of tyrosine from the body[54]. To keep the level of tyrosine in the body at a normal level, foodstuffs rich in tyrosine should be taken. Tyrosine can reduce depression, mood disorders, Parkinson's disease and in some cases Alzheimer's. Dietary sources of tyrosine are dairy products, meat, eggs, fish and oats.

Free Radicals, Oxidative Stress and Antioxidants

Our body generates free radicals, reactive oxygen species and reactive nitrogen species by various endogenous systems, exposure to different physiochemical conditions or pathological states. A balance between free radicals and antioxidants is necessary for proper physiological function. If free radicals overwhelm the body's ability to regulate them, a condition known as oxidative stress ensues. Free radicals thus adversely alter lipids, proteins and DNA, and trigger a number of human diseases. Hence application of external sources of antioxidants can assist in coping with this oxidative stress[55]. They play a part in the work of the white blood cells called phagocytes, which 'eat' bacteria and other pathogens in the body.

They also are believed to be involved in a process called redox signalling[56] where they are thought to act as cellular messengers. Free radicals are 'free' because they float around until they stabilise, and 'radical' in the sense that there are a wide variety of molecules from which they can take an electron. The damage doesn't stop there, as the new molecule, i.e. a piece of a cell wall, is now also missing an electron and has become another free radical. This snowball effect can wreak havoc on healthy tissue.

Oxidative Stress and Antioxidants

Oxidative stress means an imbalance between pro-oxidants and antioxidant mechanisms. This results in excessive oxidative metabolism. This stress can be due to several environmental factors such as exposure to pollutants, alcohol, medications, infections, poor diet, toxins, radiation etc. Oxidative damage to DNA, proteins, and other macromolecules may lead to a wide range of human diseases. (*What are Antioxidants?* Dr Ananya Mandal, MD. www.news-medical.net/health/What-are-Antioxidants.aspx)

Control of Free Radicals

Normally, various beneficial compounds known as antioxidants control free radical formation naturally. When there is deficiency of these antioxidants damage due to free radicals can become cumulative and debilitating. Antioxidants are capable of stabilising, or deactivating, free radicals before they attack cells.

Antioxidants from Food

There are several nutrients in food that contain antioxidants. Vitamin C, vitamin E and beta-carotene are among the most commonly studied dietary antioxidants.

Antioxidant Deficiencies

A diet low in fats may impair absorption of beta-carotene and vitamin E and other fat-soluble nutrients. Fruits and vegetables are important sources of vitamin C and carotenoids. Whole grains and high quality vegetable oils are major sources of vitamin E.

Many plant-derived substances are known as ‘phytonutrients’, or ‘phytochemicals’. These also possess antioxidant properties. Phenolic compounds such as flavonoids are such chemicals. They are found in fruits, vegetables and green tea extracts etc.

ALA – Alpha-lipoic Acid

Alpha-lipoic acid is an antioxidant that is made by the body and is found in every cell, where it helps turn glucose into energy. Antioxidants attack free radicals, waste products created when the body turns food into energy. Free radicals cause harmful chemical reactions that can damage cells in the body, making it harder for the body to fight off infections. They also damage organs and tissues.

When antioxidants in the body are used up as they try and get rid of free radicals, evidence suggests that alpha-lipoic acid could help regenerate other antioxidants and reactivate them again. If you are healthy, your body produces enough alpha-lipoic acid. ALA is found in red meat, organ meats (such as liver) and brewer's yeast.

Ashwagandha[57, 58, 59]

Ashwagandha is used to treat a number of disorders that affect human health including central nervous system (CNS) disorders. Ashwagandha contains many useful medicinal chemicals, including withanolides (steroidal lactones), alkaloids, choline, fatty acids, amino acids and a variety of sugars. While the leaves and fruit have valuable therapeutic properties, the root of the ashwagandha plant is the part most commonly used in Western herbal remedies. Medical researchers have been studying ashwagandha for years with great interest and have completed more than 200 studies on the healing benefits of this botanical. Adaptogens are substances (a combination of amino acids, vitamins and herbs) that modulate your response to stress or a changing environment. Adaptogens help the body cope with external stresses such as toxins in the environment, including the ability to significantly improve liver function, and it can help stabilise cortisol levels. This helps stimulate the T3 and T4 hormone synthesis (thyroid). I have made excellent progress using ashwagandha, it gives me energy and an all-over feeling of wellbeing.

Healing and Detoxing Foods

Artichokes

Artichokes help the liver function at its best, which in turn will help your body purge itself of toxins and other things it doesn't need to survive. It ups the liver's production of bile, and since bile helps break down foods, which helps your body use the nutrients inside them, an increase in bile production is typically a good thing.

Apples

Apples are full of wonderful nutrients. You get fibre, vitamins, minerals and many beneficial phytochemicals such as D-glucarate, flavonoids and terpenoids. All of these substances are used in the detox process. One flavonoid, phlorizidin, is thought to help stimulate bile production, which helps with detox as the liver gets rid of some toxins through the bile. Apples are also a good source of the soluble fibre pectin, which can help detox metals and food additives from your body. It's best to eat only organic apples as the non-organic varieties are among the top twelve foods that have been found to contain the most pesticide residues. Nevertheless I always peel them!

Almonds

Almonds are an excellent source of vitamin E. They are also high in fibre, calcium, magnesium, and useable proteins that help stabilise blood sugar. (Possible allergen.)

Asparagus

Asparagus helps to detoxify the body, it is said to help your heart stay healthy and is a general anti-inflammatory food. The second century physician Galen described asparagus as 'cleansing and healing' and research indicates that eating asparagus can act as a diuretic and possibly prevent kidney stones. According to an article titled *Chemical constituents of Asparagus*, published in the journal *Pharmacognosy Review*, asparagus helps flush out the kidneys. It has an excellent effect, I love asparagus and when it's in season I cannot get enough of it and eat it with boiled potatoes and herbs, and a little bit of melted, organic butter.

Basil

Basil has anti-bacterial properties, and is full of antioxidants to help protect the liver. The active ingredients are terpenoids. It supports the functioning of the kidneys and acts as a diuretic to help the body expel unwanted toxins.

Beetroot

A single serving of beets can do more for your health than most foods in the produce aisle. Not only can they boost your energy and lower your blood pressure, but eating beets in the long-term can help you fight cancer, reduce arthritic pain and boost your brain. Beets contain a unique mixture of natural plant chemicals (phytochemicals) and minerals that make them superb fighters of infection, blood purifiers and liver cleansers. They also help boost the body's cellular intake of oxygen, making beets excellent overall body cleansers. When you're detoxing, beets will help by making sure that the toxins you're getting out actually make it out of your body. I found that I was craving beetroot at some stage, and also drank juice from beet on a daily basis.

Broccoli

Broccoli specifically works with the enzymes in your liver to turn toxins into something your body can eliminate easily. Broccoli contains a very powerful anti-cancer, anti-diabetic and anti-microbial called sulforaphane which helps prevent cancer, diabetes, osteoporosis and allergies.

Broccoli Sprouts

Now, everybody knows how good broccoli is for you. Even better are broccoli sprouts. They are an exceptionally rich source of inducers of cellular enzymes for 'detoxifying' chemical compounds. Some of these compounds are potent enhancers of phase II enzymes, which speed up the detoxification of electrophiles and reactive oxygen metabolites. At the present time, I believe, broccoli sprouts are not being grown commercially. However, you can grow them yourself quite easily.

Burdock

Traditionally, burdock has been used as a 'blood purifier' to clear the bloodstream of toxins, as a diuretic (helping rid the body of excess water by increasing urine output), and as a topical remedy for skin problems such as eczema, acne and psoriasis. Burdock as a root vegetable possesses considerably stronger antioxidant activity than common vegetables and fruits. Recent studies confirm that burdock has pre-biotic properties that could improve health. (For supporting information see University of Maryland, 'Burdock'.) This root is a major key player in the colon cleansing kit I mention, and is part of the essiac concoction I also spoke about.

Cabbage

In addition to cleansing your liver, cabbage, especially red cabbage, will help your elimination process, which in turn helps you expel the toxins, getting them out of your system. It contains sulphur, which is essential when it comes to breaking down chemicals and removing them from your body. Cabbage is a source of an ingredient called indole-3-carbinol, which is a natural chemical that seems to boost DNA repair in cells.

Cilantro

Cilantro, also known as coriander or Chinese parsley, contains an abundance of antioxidants. Cilantro helps mobilise mercury and other metals out of the tissue so it can attach to other compounds and allow it to be excreted from the body. It also contains an antibacterial compound, which laboratory tests have shown is twice as effective as the commonly used antibiotic drugs. (See also 'Detox Herbs' further on.)

Cinnamon

Cinnamon is antimicrobial and also restrains the growth of fungi and yeast, making it potentially useful in the treatment of, for instance, allergies.

The oils from cinnamon contain active components and have been well researched. Cinnamon's essential oils also qualify it as 'antimicrobial' and have been studied for its ability to help stop the growth of bacteria as well as fungi, including the commonly problematic yeast called candida. Cinnamon has a very high antioxidant value. I have cinnamon practically every day, first thing on my porridge in the mornings. Real cinnamon is a tan colour, whereas cinnamon cassia is a reddish brown to dark brown, and has been going through the scientific press lately, mentioning too high contents of coumarin, which seemingly may be harmful. So again just pay attention to what you are buying.

Coconut Oil

Coconut oil is good for the immune system. It strengthens the immune system because it contains antimicrobial lipids, lauric acid, capric acid and caprylic acid which have antifungal, antibacterial and antiviral properties. The human body converts lauric acid into monolaurin which research has supported as an effective way to deal with viruses and bacteria that cause diseases. Coconut oil helps in fighting harmful bacteria. Liver: Medium chain triglycerides and fatty acids help in preventing liver diseases because those substances are easily converted into energy when they reach the liver, reducing the workload of the liver. They also prevent the accumulation of fat in the tissue. Saturated fatty acids: Most of them are medium chain triglycerides, which are said to assimilate well in the body's systems. Lauric acid is the main contributor, and represents more than forty percent of the total, followed by capric acid, caprylic acid, myristic acid and palmitic acid. I know of some crew members who have noticed huge improvements by using coconut oil in high doses in connection with a 'ketogenic' diet (high in fat). The fat used is a high dose of clean cholesterol, known as medium chain triglycerides. I have tried this (just the coconut oil, not the ketogenic diet itself) in addition to using high doses of krill oil (3x2 capsules per day) and noticed big improvements in my brain function.

Cranberries

While they are more popular as fruits that help prevent urinary tract infections, cranberries are antibacterial and are known to remove many different toxins from your body. Cranberries feature a rich profile of anti-inflammatory nutrients, provide immune and cardiovascular support, as well as promote digestive and bladder/kidney health. Do not use the usually sweetened (added sugars) cranberry juices!

Dandelion Leaves

Dandelions are considered a powerhouse food full of nutrients that are essential for anyone. Dandelion root is known to act on the liver and pancreas as it helps strain and filter toxins and wastes from the bloods and it has beneficial effects on liver complaints which have been well documented by both Asian practitioners and Western medicine physicians. They are a rich source of minerals and provide a variety of phytonutrients. They have a high source of super-antioxidants that support the cleansing of the digestive tract. Try adding dandelion leaves (rucola) to your salad. I always add handfuls to pasta dishes and rice meals just stirring under when the food is ready so they don't lose their healthy properties. If you live in the country you can pick fresh dandelion leaves, but pick young leaves and wash well of course. The dandelion leaves will have a more bitter taste than rucola. Chop and dry them and make a tea, 1 cup every morning, instead or as a change from stinging nettle tea (not longer than 21 days, then take a break).

Fennel

The fennel bulb is high in fibre. In addition to its fibre, fennel is a very good source of folate, a B-vitamin that is necessary for the conversion of a dangerous molecule called homocysteine into other benign molecules. Potassium, found in high levels in fennel bulbs and seeds, is an electrolyte, which means that it facilitates increased electrical conduction throughout the body. This includes connections within the brain, which is a veritable switchboard of electric currents. Potassium can help increase brain function and cognitive abilities through this quality. Fennel is a vasodilator, which means more oxygen reaches the brain through which neural activity can work more effectively.

Flaxseed

When detoxifying your body, it is essential to ensure toxins are eliminated properly. Ground flaxseed provides a wonderful source of fibre that helps to bind and flush toxins from the intestinal tract and colon. They are also an excellent source of omega-3 oils. Try consuming two tablespoons of ground flaxseed in lemon water every morning or sprinkle it over your porridge.

Garlic

Many detox diets list garlic as a crucial piece of the puzzle. The reason is that garlic boosts the immune system as well as helping out the liver. One good thing about garlic is that you can up your intake without having to worry if your body is going to get used to it or build up a resistance, although it might be so effective that it could drop your blood pressure if it is low already, which happened to me and made me feel very ill. Sulphur is found in high quantities in garlic, which makes it a good detox food and its antibiotic properties help heal your body.

Ginger

Alongside turmeric, ginger is one of the most potent disease-fighting plants. Ginger has broad-spectrum antibacterial, antiviral, antioxidant and anti-parasitic properties. In 2013, a study also found that female athletes who took three grams of ginger or cinnamon every day had a significant decrease in achy muscles. The pain-relieving potential of ginger appears to be far-reaching. Along with help for muscle and joint pain, ginger has been found to help the severity of migraine headaches and the queasiness when pregnant or other forms of nausea.

Goji Berries

Unique among fruits because they contain all essential amino acids, goji berries also have the highest concentration of protein of any fruit. They are loaded with vitamin C, and contain more carotenoids than any other food; they have twenty-one trace minerals. Boasting 15 times the amount of iron found in the famous spinach, they also have calcium, zinc, selenium and many other important trace minerals and with all that there is no doubt that they are a nutritional powerhouse.

In traditional Chinese medicine, the goji is said to act on the kidney and liver meridians and to help with lower back pain, dizziness and eyesight. They are most often consumed raw, made into a tea or extract, or as an ingredient in soups.

Green Tea

Green tea is a great addition to any detox programme because of its high antioxidant value. It is the least processed tea and provides the most antioxidant polyphenols, which are believed to be responsible for most of the health benefits linked to green tea along with two widely studied compounds found almost exclusively in green tea which are: epigallocatechin gallate (EGCG) and L-theanine[60]. The Memorial Sloan Kettering Cancer Center lists L-theanine benefits as having anti-tumour, anti-obesity and neuroprotective agents against stroke and Alzheimer's. It is said that L-theanine increases levels of the neurotransmitters serotonin, dopamine and GABA, thus improving recall, learning, and positive mood. Another part of the body that responds positively to theanine[60] is the liver.

It won't suffice to drink several cups of green tea though, but I have been taking green tea capsules for a very long time now and find them very beneficial. (Please also refer to 'Herbal Teas' further on.)

Kale

Kale helps the detoxification system. New research has shown that the ITCs (isothiocyanates) made from kale's glucosinolates can help regulate detox at a genetic level. This vegetable is so good for you that it is often recommended to patients that are following a doctor-recommended diet when fighting kidney or liver disease. It's packed with so many antioxidants and has anti-inflammatory properties as well, not to mention all of the vitamins and minerals it contains. Leafy greens are likely the number one food you can eat to regularly help improve your health. They're filled with fibre along with important vitamins, minerals and plant-based phytochemicals that can help protect you from diseases. I love kale and cook it with other vegetables, then eat it along with steamed potatoes or rice, or use it in my green juices.

Lemon Grass

This is a herb that is used as a natural way to cleanse several organs at once. It not only helps the liver but also the kidneys, the bladder and the entire digestive tract. (Please refer to 'Herbal Teas' further on.)

Lemons

This wonderful fruit stimulates the release of enzymes and helps convert toxins into a water-soluble form that can be easily excreted from the body. In addition, they contain high amounts of vitamin C, a vitamin needed by the body to make glutathione. Glutathione helps ensure that Phase II liver detoxification keeps up with Phase I, helping to reduce the likelihood of negative effects from chemicals. Drinking lemon water, which is alkaline-forming, first thing in the morning will help balance out acidity build up. They also have an excellent effect in detoxing the liver. I drink the juice of at least one lemon every day in my water.

Olive Oil

Some liver cleanses out there call for olive oil mixed with grapefruit juice and Epsom salt (see 'Liver Cleanse') in order to trigger your liver to expel gallstones. Your best choice is unrefined olive oil, which does not undergo chemical refining. 'Extra virgin' olive oil should have the aroma of olives but it can also have the fragrance of simply ripe olives. The slightest hint of mustiness or metallic smell is a sign that something is wrong and you must not use it. Another tip from me: Check the source and do not save money on this product. Cheap oils are often mixes!

Onions

This unassuming kitchen staple is as healthy as it is tasty. It's brimming with sulphur-containing amino acids, which efficiently detox the liver. Raw onions deliver the most health benefits. The total polyphenol content of onion is not only higher than its fellow allium vegetables, garlic and leeks, but also higher than tomatoes, carrots and red bell pepper. Onions have been shown to inhibit the activity of macrophages, specialised white blood cells that play a key role in our body's immune defence system, and one of their defence activities involves the triggering of large-scale inflammatory responses. My grandmother taught me my first lessons with onions, using poultices on my chest, and she made me inhale onion steam when I had colds, eat onion pie and onion soup, and she made onion syrup to sooth sore throats.

Seaweed

Seaweed may be the most underrated vegetable in the Western world. Studies at McGill University in Montreal showed that seaweeds bind to radioactive waste in the body so it can be removed. Radioactive waste can find its way into the body through some medical tests or through food that has been grown where water or soil is contaminated. Radioactivity is something aviators are exposed to every day they fly! Seaweed also binds to heavy metals to help eliminate them from the body. In addition, it is a powerhouse of minerals and trace minerals. But, always check where it is from – you don't want pre-contaminated seaweed!

Turmeric[61, 62]

Curcumin, the compound that gives turmeric its yellow colour, is a very interesting product because it inhibits Phase I while stimulating Phase II detox. The rate at which your detox pathways function depends on your genes, your age, your lifestyle and of a good supply of nutrients during the detox process. Curcumin is used a lot in Ayurvedic medicine to treat liver and digestive disorders. Turmeric has specifically been studied and extensively so in relation to the positive effect that it has on the liver. Curcumin seems to be a potent antioxidant that can neutralise free radicals due to its chemical structure. As a high antioxidant spice, turmeric protects the body and helps prevent disease. Curcumin also boosts the activity of the body's own antioxidant enzymes. It is important to know that one must take Curcumin together with piperine (or black pepper) to activate the metabolising process, otherwise most of the goodness in the Curcumin is simply unrecognised by the system and goes straight out again. Literally hundreds of studies have been conducted with, to my knowledge, all positive results! I take it in capsule form regularly plus of course in my curries.

Watercress

Give your liver a big boost with the cleansing action of watercress, which can be added to each and every salad you make. When you're making smoothies for your detoxing this is a great green to blend in with others. It helps to release enzymes in the liver that help it get rid of toxic build-up.

Wheat grass[63, 64]

Clinical studies have confirmed that wheat grass juice and wheat grass extract have healing properties. Wheat grass juice's abundance of alkaline minerals helps reduce over-acidity in the blood and is a powerful detoxifier and liver protector. It also cleanses the organs and gastrointestinal tract of mucous plaque. Wheat grass stimulates the metabolism and the body's enzyme systems. It also helps reduce blood pressure. Nutritionally, wheat grass is a complete food that contains huge amounts of earth elements. I take one frozen dose every morning, definitely one of the best things I discovered on my journey to better health and detox! You can easily grow it yourself. If you buy frozen wheat grass, make sure how they freeze it (shock freezing) so it has as many of the nutrients left as possible.

Healthy Proteins

There are plenty of reasons to eat more meat-free meals: they are nearly always cheaper, lower in calories, and better for the environment, never mind the fact of them being easier on your system.

It's easy to get enough protein without eating animals, but doubters often have another concern: are these meat-free protein sources complete? The term complete protein refers to amino acids, the building blocks of protein. There are twenty different amino acids that can form a protein, and nine that the body can't produce on its own. These are called essential amino acids – we need to eat them because we can't make them ourselves. In order to be considered 'complete', a protein must contain all nine of these essential amino acids in roughly equal amounts.

Yes, meat and eggs are complete proteins, and beans and nuts aren't. But humans don't need every essential amino acid in every bite of food in every meal they eat; we only need a sufficient amount of each amino acid every day. But even then, if we go one day without one or the other building block (amino acid) we usually do not crumble to pieces.

The following are excellent protein sources:

Quinoa

This protein-packed grain contains every amino acid, and is

particularly rich in lysine, which promotes healthy tissue growth throughout the body. Quinoa is also a good source of iron, magnesium, vitamin E, potassium and fibre. It looks a bit like couscous and is as versatile as rice, but quinoa has a richer, nuttier flavour than either of them.

Buckwheat[65]

Many people think that buckwheat is a cereal grain; it is actually related to rhubarb and sorrel, making it an excellent substitute for grains for people who are sensitive to wheat or other grains that contain protein glutens. Also, buckwheat flowers are wonderfully fragrant and are very attractive to bees that use them to produce a strongly flavoured, dark honey. Buckwheat is also a good source of magnesium.

Hempseed

Hemp is a high protein seed containing all nine of the essential amino acids (like flax). It also has high amounts of fatty acids and fibre as well as vitamin E and trace minerals. It has a well-balanced ratio of omega-3 to -6 fats, and is a great replacement for those who do not wish to use krill or fish oil for the omega-3 contents.

Chia

Chia is an edible seed that comes from a Mexican desert plant. 'Chia' means strength, and legend has it that the cultures in South America used the tiny black and white seeds as an energy booster. That makes sense, since chia seeds are a highly concentrated food containing the very much needed omega-3 fatty acids, fibre, antioxidants and calcium.

Soy

Soy is a legume and used in tofu, soy milk and as a dairy and meat substitute. It is also used in fermented foods such as miso, natto and tempeh, which are a staple in Asian countries. Over 90 percent of soy is produced in the U.S.A. and, as seems, is genetically modified; it has been widely reported that the crops are sprayed with the herbicide Roundup, the most widely used herbicide in the world, with glyphosate[66, 67], the active ingredient which was classified as 'probably carcinogenic to humans', which was released in a report on Friday, 21st March, 2015 by cancer researchers who are affiliated with the World Health Organisation[66].

Whole soybeans contain large amounts of manganese, selenium, copper, potassium, phosphorus, magnesium, iron, calcium, vitamins B6, B2 and B1, and vitamin K. Whole soybeans are rich in micro-nutrients, but they also contain phytates which block absorption of minerals.

I do not do well on soy products anymore, so I limit its intake to a few times per month. I am not sure if it might be because I managed to get 'sprayed' soy products, or if it is for another reason. Of course, if you do well with it, please add it to your food plan, two to three times a week. Please make sure it is GMO and pesticide and herbicide free! Do not use soy oil at all for this reason.

Microprotein (Quorn)

This also does not agree with my system anymore; it can be due to an allergen such as egg, milk and gluten; please check it out and try for yourself. I did very well with it for a long time, but when my health got worse after the second poisoning I couldn't eat it any more.

Both soy and quorn would be good protein sources and meat replacements.

Rice

Arsenic warnings are going around like wild fire! Rice tends to absorb arsenic more readily than many other plants. Arsenic has two chemical forms, inorganic and organic (the latter of which can be less toxic), and is naturally part of the minerals in the earth's crust. (Note, organic is a chemistry term and should not be confused with food sold as 'organic'.) Arsenic also has been released into the environment through the use of pesticides and poultry fertiliser. Therefore, it's in soil and water. Make sure you can determine the source where the rice came from.

Beans

More than just a meat substitute, beans are so nutritious that the latest dietary guidelines recommend we triple our current intake from one to three portions per week. This difference in fibre content means that meat is digested fairly quickly whereas beans are digested slowly, keeping you satisfied longer. Plus, beans are low in sugar, which prevents insulin in the bloodstream from spiking, causing hunger. When you substitute beans for meat in your diet, you get the added bonus of a decrease in saturated fat. (*Eat right, Feel awesome*, D. J. Blatner.) Rice and beans in a meal together have the same protein as meat.

Lentils

Lentils are the non-meat source of iron. Iron deficiency is the most common nutritional disorder in the world, according to the World Health Organisation. Not getting enough iron in your diet can deplete your stores and cause you to feel weak and tired. Lentils are a good source of iron, with 3.3 milligrams in a ½-cup serving. However, your body can't absorb as much of the iron from plant-based lentils as it does from meat sources. Eating your lentils with a food rich in vitamin C, such as peppers, can help improve absorption. I even found lentil flour based pasta and pancake mix, and love it!

About Salt

Salt is not only critical to your life, but it is one of the basic elements which your body needs. The relationship between salt and your health is so intricately involved as to make them impossible to be disentangled. Without salt, you could not exist.

Essentially, every cell in the human body is dependent on the presence of sodium. We find sodium diffused throughout the fluid between cells. Each cell in our body is like a small ocean containing salty water. Inside our cells we find primarily potassium. These two minerals, sodium and potassium, need to be in constant, dynamic balance so the cells can exchange incoming energy with outgoing, depleted energy. Salt increases conductivity in nerve cells for communication and information processing. It enhances the absorption of nutrients through the intestinal tract. It helps clear mucous plugs and sticky phlegm in the lungs, particularly in asthma, and it helps clear up congestion of the sinuses. To name just a few benefits. But, and again a word of caution, this does not mean that you should use excess amounts of salt and, when you do, use high quality salts like Himalaya salt or unwashed sea salt (unprocessed without added chemicals, iodine and moisture absorbents etc.). If to date you have refrained from all salt, try and introduce that bit into your daily diet, you will notice a difference. I did. There are a massive amount of studies that contradict the notion that salt raises blood pressure and causes other illnesses.

Nuts and Seeds

Almonds

They are packed with vitamins, minerals, protein and fibre, and are associated with a number of health benefits. Just a handful of almonds, approximately one ounce, contain one-eighth of our necessary daily protein. Almonds are a source of vitamin E, copper, magnesium and high quality protein. There are potential risks associated with the consumption of almonds. Allergy to almonds is actually rather common, so you might want to get that tested if you are worried about it.

Almonds may be eaten on their own, raw or toasted. They are also the ingredients of several different dishes. Almonds are available sliced, flaked, slivered, as flour, oil, butter, or as almond milk. I love almond butter and almond milk.

Brazil Nuts

These tasty treats are packed with selenium, which is key to flushing mercury out of your body. The body uses selenium to make 'selenoproteins', which work like antioxidants preventing damage to cells and there is a growing body of evidence to show it has a key role in our health. Four to five Brazil nuts a day they say, covers your selenium.

Cedar Nuts/Pine Nuts

Cedar nuts contain a complex of B vitamins, which normalise the activity of the nervous system. They are a source of micro-nutrients such as copper, cobalt, manganese and zinc. As the richest source of lecithin they are comparable only to soybean. Cedar nuts are also a rich source of iodine.

Cashews

Are rich in minerals like copper, magnesium, zinc, iron and biotin. They are actually a low-fat nut and, like olive oil, they have a high concentration of oleic acid. According to Dr Andrew Saul, one big handful of cashews provides one to two thousand milligrams of tryptophan, which will work as well as prescription antidepressant.

Hazelnuts

Are rich in vitamins B1, B2, B3, B5, B6 and B9. We rely on the B vitamins to dismantle proteins, fats and carbohydrates, thereby providing us with the energy we need to function. Our nervous system needs amino acids in order to function, and amino acids require vitamin B6. Hazelnuts are rich in vitamin B6. Moreover, vitamin B6 is necessary for the creation of myelin, the insulating sheath of the nerve that increases the speed and efficiency of electrical impulses, allowing the nervous system to operate optimally. Allergy to hazelnut is often found in patients with hay fever (allergic rhino-conjunctivitis) and tree pollen allergy.

Walnuts

Walnuts are extremely good for your heart and brain. Pecans have loads of vitamins and minerals like vitamins E and A, folic acid, calcium, magnesium, copper, phosphorus, potassium, manganese, B vitamins and zinc.

Peanuts

Peanuts are not actually nuts, they are legumes. For people with nut allergies, the distinction is particularly important, since many individuals with nut allergies can eat peanuts safely. Conversely, people who are allergic to peanuts can often eat nuts. They are a plant protein and a rich source of minerals like magnesium, phosphorus, potassium, zinc, calcium, sodium, etc. A peanut allergy is perhaps the most serious food allergy you can develop. Peanut allergy sufferers are at high risk of serious allergic reactions that can actually be life threatening, even if the first episode of peanut sensitivity was not severe. If you suspect you have a peanut allergy, you need to get tested by an allergist immediately and avoid all nut products until the allergy is determined as legitimate or not.

Peanuts are susceptible to contamination of aflatoxin produced by a fungus, aspergillus flavus, which is very toxic.

Peanut butter

It's packed with nutrition. A serving of peanut butter has the powerful antioxidant vitamin E, bone-building magnesium, muscle-friendly potassium, and immunity-boosting vitamin B6. Research shows that eating peanuts can decrease your risk of heart disease, diabetes and other chronic health conditions. One study published in the *Journal of the American Medical Association* found that consuming 1 ounce of nuts or peanut butter (about two tablespoons) at least five days a week can lower the risk of developing diabetes by almost 30 percent. It's got the good fat – peanut butter is chock-full of heart-healthy monounsaturated fat. Attention: possible peanut allergies!

Thank goodness I am only slightly allergic to hazelnuts!

Here are the healthiest seeds:

Flaxseeds

Flaxseeds are definitely at the top of my list, especially if you do not want to use krill oil. Two tablespoons of ground flaxseed per day is ideal and easy to add to porridge or smoothies. Cold-pressed organic flax oil is the best source of parent omega-3s (better than fish oil, also because fish oil can be contaminated).

Hemp seeds

Hemp seeds are a certified super food. They are high in protein and fibre (excellent for sluggish digestion), with balanced omega-3 and -6 fatty acids. I also add one to two tablespoons to my salads or in my porridge.

Sunflower seeds

Sunflower seeds also help prevent heart disease and cancer with phytochemicals, folate, vitamin E, selenium and copper. Don't eat them raw; grill or bake them until they turn light brown

Pumpkin seeds

Pumpkin seeds are great for your immune system with lots of antioxidants (carotenoids), omega-3 fatty acids and zinc.

Sesame seeds

Sesame seeds are a good source of calcium, magnesium, zinc, fibre, iron, B1 and phosphorus. They can lower blood pressure and protect against liver damage. Sesame seeds have also been linked to prevention of many diseases like arthritis, asthma, migraine headaches, menopause, osteoporosis and may even reduce PMS symptoms. **Tahini** is a ground sesame seed paste that's a popular ingredient in Middle Eastern dishes we eat, like houmous.

Apricot seeds

Apricot seeds (aka apricot kernels), apple seeds and other bitter fruit seeds contain amygdalin (aka vitamin B17), which has incredibly powerful anti-cancer properties.

Houmous

One of the healthier options for dips is the Middle Eastern houmous made with chickpeas, olive oil, garlic, lemon juice and tahini, which is a sesame seed paste (see above). It provides you with protein and a number of essential vitamins and minerals. Each serving of houmous provides folate, as well as small amounts of vitamin A, thiamine, riboflavin, niacin and vitamin B6. Folate is essential for producing new cells, including red blood cells and DNA.

Note: if you are not sure if you have a nut allergy, particularly to peanuts and hazelnuts, get it tested!

Fruit

Mangoes

Mangoes can help to alkalinise the whole body by helping to flush out toxic acids and rebuild the alkaline reserves. Mangoes are packed with enzymes and are a pro-biotic food, meaning they contain compounds that stimulate and feed the good bacteria in the intestines which greatly aids in digestion and assimilation. Mangoes contain a significant amount of pyridoxine (B6), which is vital for the synthesis of serotonin and dopamine in the brain. In some countries mangoes are eaten right before bed as a natural sleep aid.

Vanilla Beans

Vanilla beans are a highly prized medicinal fruit of the vanilla *planifolia* orchid and have several health promoting properties. Vanilla has a calming effect on the nervous system and is an effective treatment for anxiety and stress. The aroma of vanilla beans alone has been shown to increase feelings of relaxation and happiness. One of the major medicinal compounds in vanilla beans is called vanillin, which in small doses is known to greatly aid digestion, decrease headaches and provide relief for an upset stomach. Vanilla beans contain trace minerals such as zinc, iron, calcium, magnesium and iron. They also contain anti-inflammatory and pain-relieving properties and are particularly beneficial for fatigue, muscle and joint pain, neck and back pain, nausea and swelling.

Blackberries

Blackberries are nutritionally packed with vitamins C, E, A and K, minerals magnesium, potassium, manganese, copper, and antioxidants such as ellagic acid. Blackberries contain powerful anti-carcinogenic agents making them one of the top ORAC fruits available and one of the best fruits to eat to help prevent cancer. The anthocyanins in blackberries (which give them their dark colour) have the ability to significantly reduce inflammation, which benefits autoimmune diseases and cardiovascular diseases.

Avocados

This wonderful fruit is packed with antioxidants, helps lower cholesterol and dilates the blood vessels while blocking artery-destroying toxicity. Avocados contain the nutrient called glutathione, which blocks at least thirty different carcinogens, while helping the liver detoxify synthetic chemicals. I love avocados, either with a sprinkle of salt or vinaigrette or just on a slice of wheat-free bread or rye Knäckebrot.

Bananas

Bananas are one of the most nutritional and healing fruits readily available today. They are 76 percent water and are packed with vitamins, such as vitamins C and B6, and minerals such as potassium, copper and manganese. This high water/nutrient ratio makes them a great electrolyte food. Bananas are also an excellent 'brain food', great for heavy thinkers and are known to help strengthen the nervous system. Bananas contain powerful anti-fungal and antibiotic compounds as well as protease inhibitors, which can help stop viruses in their tracts. A banana a day...

Melons

Melons are an amazing fruit that has over 19 vitamins and minerals that help to boost the immune system, detoxify the organs, and deeply hydrate and alkalinise the body. Since melon is a pre-digested food, meaning it does not require any digestion in the stomach and can pass straight through to the intestines for assimilation, it is best eaten on an empty stomach alone for breakfast. The high vitamin C content in melons is critical for immune system support and to fight bacterial and viral infections.

Cherries

Cherries are a medicinal powerhouse fruit that are packed with vitamins A, C and E, and minerals such as iron, copper, zinc, potassium and manganese. The high levels of anthocyanins and antioxidants found in cherries make them an excellent food to help the body fight against neurological diseases, diabetes, and cancers.

Grapes

Grapes have been called the 'queen of fruits' due to being one of the most nutritious and medicinal foods available since ancient times. Grapes are a rich source of vitamins A, C and B-complex, and minerals such as calcium, magnesium, copper, boron, manganese, iron, selenium and potassium. Grapes contain high amounts of powerful antioxidants known as bioflavonoids, resveratrol and anthocyanins. These phytochemicals are anti-inflammatory, anti-viral, anti-microbial, anti-aging and anti-cancerous, and provide protection against anaemia, degenerative nerve diseases, heart disease, viral and fungal infection. Please wash and dry them very well, they are heavily sprayed; try to get organically grown grapes!

Please be careful with berries in general, they easily turn blue-mouldy. Some moulds can cause allergic reactions and respiratory problems, and some in the right conditions produce mycotoxins, which are poisonous substances that can make you sick.

Wheat and the Gluten Scare

Many demonise wheat gluten these days, but with the obvious exceptions of sufferers and the gluten intolerant people, it is nothing to be afraid of, but you must make sure it is organically grown. Standard wheat harvest protocol in the United States is to drench the wheat fields with 'Roundup' several days before the harvesters work through the fields, as withered, dead wheat plants are less taxing on the farm equipment and allows for an earlier, easier and bigger harvest. Pre-harvest application of the herbicide Roundup (please refer to above-mentioned article under 'Soy') and other herbicides containing the deadly active ingredient glyphosate to wheat and barley as a desiccant was suggested as early as 1980. In synergy with (the) disruption of the biosynthesis of important amino acids via the shikimate pathway, glyphosate (active ingredient in Roundup) inhibits the cytochrome P450 (CYP) enzymes produced by the gut micro-biome. (Source: *The Healthy Home Economist* and Dr Stephanie Seneff)[9]

Carbohydrates

I have never been a fan of low-carb diets. Carbohydrates have been given a bad reputation, which is wrong! Our bodies and brains need carbohydrates to work effectively. Of course, not all carbohydrates are good.

First of all, fruits, dairy and vegetables are all sources of carbohydrates. And when it comes to starches, there are indeed good carbs and the bad, for instance cakes, biscuits, white breads etc.

Eating good carbs in place of refined ones can reduce your risk of the diseases that can be caused by bad carbs (diabetes, heart disease etc.). A study published in the *Journal of Nutrition* found that eating three servings of whole grains a day helped people reduce their total body fat and abdominal fat.

Whole-grain foods, especially those without added sugars, are good carbohydrates because they are high in fibre and nutrients. The healthiest sources of carbohydrates, unprocessed or minimally processed whole grains, vegetables, fruits and beans, promote good health by delivering vitamins, minerals, fibre and a host of important phytonutrients.

Try this for adding healthy carbohydrates to your detox programme/diet:

Start the day with whole grains. Try a hot cereal, like steel cut or old-fashioned oats (not instant oatmeal), or a cold cereal (organic) that lists a whole grain first on the ingredient list and has no added sugar.

Whole Grains

Studies show that eating whole grains instead of refined grains lowers the risk of many chronic diseases. While benefits are most pronounced for those consuming at least three servings daily, some studies show reduced risks from as little as one serving daily. The message: every whole grain in your diet helps! The bran and fibre in whole grains make it more difficult for digestive enzymes to break down the starches into glucose. I rinse all grains well under warm water before cooking them; it helps remove some of the starch.

If you can't resist eating bread, use whole grain breads for lunch or snacks. Are you confused about how to find whole grain bread? Look for bread that lists as the first ingredient whole wheat, whole rye, or some other grain, and states that there are no added sugars, preservatives or colourants – and even better, one that is made with whole grains. Even better than that, bake your bread yourself, it's easy enough!

Instead of bread, try a whole grain in salad such as brown rice, couscous or quinoa. Pass once in a while on potatoes, and instead bring on the beans. Beans and other legumes such as chickpeas provide a healthy dose of protein.

Choose whole fruit instead of pre-fabricated juice. Or juice fresh fruit yourself, which I have recommended elsewhere to do anyway once, if not twice a day, as your all green power drink!

Dairy Products

Although not typically considered carbohydrate foods, dairy products do contain some carbohydrates in the form of lactose, a type of sugar. As long as you choose dairy products without added sugars, such as plain (raw) milk, yoghurt or kefir. Kefir is a unique cultured dairy product that is one of the most pro-biotic rich foods on the planet and has incredible medicinal benefits for healing issues like leaky gut. Its unique name comes from the Turkish word 'keif', which means 'good feeling'. These would be good carbohydrates, except if you know that you are lactose intolerant – do get at test done if you are not sure, otherwise you might miss out on some lovely dishes thinking you are lactose intolerant when in fact you are not! If possible, stay off too much dairy, since it can clog the system, as mentioned before. The casein in cows' milk can clog and irritate the body's entire respiratory system. Dairy products are implicated in almost all respiratory problems. I noticed a big improvement when I refrained from eating these products; I used to be a big cheese and yoghurt eater! I took a long break from these products, and am at the moment re-introducing some, only organic, little by little...

Sweeteners

Refined sugar is definitely considered a 'bad' carbohydrate. Use good organic honey. The main thing to remember when it comes to honey is that not all honey is created equal. Your average domestic 'Grade A' type honey found in the supermarket is likely highly processed and full with sugar. Unrefined honey contains an abundance of various antioxidants that can have major implications for health. Manuka honey is expensive, yes, but is said to have antibacterial and a natural antibiotic effect.

Studies have revealed that e.g. the consumption of buckwheat honey increases the antioxidant value of the blood. You could replace refined sugar with an identical amount of maple syrup, which will cut the total sugar content by a third. Avoid at all cost high fructose corn syrup.

Potatoes

One large spud baked with the skin on contains about 1,600 milligrams of potassium, nearly half the recommended amount for an entire day and almost four times as much as a medium banana, famous for its potassium content. It is an essential electrolyte key to hydration and has lots of fibre. They also have plenty of manganese and vitamins B6 and C. I eat lots of spuds! Mainly boiled, then I might add avocado (guacamole) and lots of fresh chopped herbs and some organic butter or coconut oil, or I add curry instead of herbs with a side salad. There are plenty of varieties. In Germany you can go to the 'Kartoffel Hotel' – the 'Potato Hotel'; I think they used to offer only potato dishes, nowadays it's 'mainly' potato dishes and they use them in their wellness department as wraps too, that's how good potatoes are for you!

Bad Carbs

- Sugar is in practically everything ready-made!
- White flour
- White bread
- White flour pasta
- White rice
- Bread rolls
- Croissants
- Burger buns
- Tortillas and wraps
- Breadcrumbs

- Bread sticks
- Cookies and biscuits
- Pizza dough

Detox Herbs

I am a herb lover, and believe in their healthy properties and health benefits! I will drink any herb as a 'tisane' or 'infusion', mix various herbs and flowers and will also use them as a poultice or in the sauna in the water for steam. My grandparents taught me herbal uses when they started taking me on mountain tours as a toddler; I used to sit in the hay-basket on granddad's back, and they taught me while gathering wild herbs!

You can grow them yourself, even without a garden, on your windowsill or in your kitchen. I have listed a few here. If you are interested in more information you can always Google them and find well-documented articles and even scientific studies about these particular plants.

Bitter herbs help improve Phase I and II detoxification. Bitter herbs are the cornerstone of herbal medicine. A range of physiological responses occur following stimulation of the bitter receptors of the tongue. The bitter taste stimulates the specific bitter taste buds at the back of the tongue to stimulate the parasympathetic nervous system to trigger a number of reflexes. These reflexes are important to the digestive process and general health.

Parsley

Those pretty green leaves don't just make your plate look nice. Parsley boasts a huge amount of beta-carotene and vitamins A, C and K to protect your kidneys and bladder. A diuretic herb, parsley can help prevent problems such as kidney stones and bladder infections and keep our body's 'plumbing' running smoothly by causing it to produce more urine. The flavonoids in parsley have been shown to function as antioxidants that combine with highly reactive oxygen-containing molecules (called oxygen radicals) and help prevent lack of oxygen-based damage to cells. In addition, extracts from parsley have been used in (animal) studies to help increase the antioxidant capacity of the blood. I love a pile of fresh chopped parsley on boiled potatoes or a slice of organic homemade bread with butter and on my big bowls of mixed salads. It grows easily and makes a lovely decoration plant too!

Dandelion

Dandelion is a mild bitter herb used as a blood cleanser and diuretic, which is also said to lower cholesterol and blood pressure (see page 162).

Yarrow

Yarrow is a flowering plant that produces a mild bitter herb used as an astringent and cold remedy. The entire herb can be used.

Milk Thistle

Milk thistle, also a bitter herb, helps with general liver problems including jaundice, hepatic pain and swelling. Flavonoids discovered in milk thistle seed add to the significant liver regenerating and protecting qualities found in other parts of milk thistle. Flavonoids contained in the herb help stabilise cell membranes and control cell function. Milk thistle is also thought to be beneficial for the following problems: acute viral hepatitis, metabolic disease, continual-persistent hepatitis and cirrhosis of the liver.

Cilantro (Coriander)

Cilantro, bitter, is instrumental in helping the body rid itself of dangerous toxic metals that accumulate in organ tissues. The herb is a good source of minerals like potassium, calcium, manganese, iron and magnesium. Potassium is an important component of cell and body fluids that helps control heart rate and blood pressure. Iron is essential for red blood cell production.

It is also rich in many vital vitamins, including folic acid, riboflavin, niacin, vitamin A, beta-carotene and vitamin C, which are essential for optimum health. Vitamin C is a powerful natural antioxidant.

Peppermint

Peppermint also belongs to the bitter herbs and has a soothing quality that helps with coughing associated with colds and flu. Peppermint oil can relax the smooth muscles of the GI tract, which is why it is so commonly a component of 'over-the-counter' medications. A number of studies have also shown it to be a great reliever of irritable bowel syndrome. Peppermint oil is very helpful as an aid for digestion. People often put a few drops of peppermint oil in a glass of water and drink it after their meal for its beneficial digestive properties. Peppermint oil is also a good tonic for those who have a low appetite, and it helps in treating motion sickness, nausea and upset stomachs.

Eucalyptus

Eucalyptus is another bitter herb that helps with lung cleansing. Eucalyptus essential oil is effective for treating a number of respiratory problems including cold, cough, runny nose, sore throat, asthma, nasal congestion, bronchitis and sinusitis. Eucalyptus oil is antibacterial, anti-fungal, antimicrobial, antiviral, anti-inflammatory and decongestant in nature, which makes it a good ingredient in many medicines that treat respiratory problems. One very important reason that many people use eucalyptus oil is that it creates a cooling and refreshing effect. Normally, people suffering from certain conditions and disorders are slightly sluggish. Eucalyptus oil removes exhaustion, mental sluggishness and rejuvenates the spirits of the sick. It can also be effective in the treatment of stress. Aside from mental exhaustion, eucalyptus essential oil is commonly used to stimulate mental activity and increase blood flow to the brain.

Stinging Nettle

Stinging nettle is known for its ability to resist microorganisms; it also possesses antioxidant properties. Taken as a tea, it has been found to help cure mucus congestion, skin irritations, water retention and diarrhoea. The beverage also helps stimulate the digestive glands of the stomach, intestines, liver, pancreas and gall bladder. Applied externally, nettle tea may relieve rheumatism in both people and animals, and makes a first-class gargle for mouth and throat infections; it helps to clear up acne and eczema and promotes the healing of burns.

Sarsaparilla

Sarsaparilla has detoxifying and anti-inflammatory properties, and contains saponins, which act as a diuretic, and it is used to promote healthy kidney functioning by stimulating detoxification through forced urination.

Slightly bitter sarsaparilla binds with toxins and is used to improve liver function and cleanse the blood.

Herbal Tisanes and Infusions

Green Tea

Green tea is loaded with polyphenols like flavonoids and catechins, which function as powerful antioxidants.

These substances can reduce the formation of free radicals in the body, protecting cells and molecules from damage. These free radicals are known to play a role in ageing and all sorts of diseases. One of the more powerful compounds in green tea is the antioxidant epigallocatechin gallate (EGCG), which has been studied to treat various diseases and may be one of the main reasons green tea has such powerful medicinal properties. Also, a compound called L-theanine has been studied extensively. It can also cross the blood-brain barrier intact, and register pharmacological effects directly. Theanine has been reported to raise levels of brain serotonin, dopamine and GABA, with possible improvement in specific memory and learning tasks. Green tea also has small amounts of minerals that are important for health. If you are coming off coffee, you could substitute the 'missing' caffeine with green tea! Personally I even take green tea capsules daily due to the high effect of green tea in protecting cells and the effects from the ingredient L-theanine[60] are very noticeable. It also seems to help calm brain waves; it helped me sleep over a very long period of time.

White Tea

White tea is higher in antioxidants than most other teas. When brewed at a low temperature it's also lower in caffeine than most teas. It has a very mellow flavour that appeals to some detoxers.

Rooibos

Rooibos is high in antioxidants. Flavour-wise, a great substitute for black tea or coffee. It's also easy to blend with other flavours, including many of the detoxifying spices and herbs in this list. Rooibos is caffeine free.

Ginger

Ginger has long been considered to be warming, cleansing and beneficial to digestion, and a diuretic. It's also enjoyable to drink. Some add lemon juice or zest to their ginger 'tea'. Ginger also tastes great with masala chai (tea) spices.

Masala Chai Spices

Many masala chai spices (such as ginger, cloves, cardamom, cinnamon and black pepper) are considered to be detoxifying. Try making masala chai without milk or sugar for the most potential benefit. If you want to avoid caffeine, skip the black tea and boil the spices for an antioxidant-rich, flavourful decoction, which you could also mix with Rooibos tea.

Peppermint

Peppermint invigorates without caffeine, so it's great for those who are trying to reduce or eliminate caffeine in their diet.

Some say it is cleansing, and traditionally it's used to aid in digestion. If you like peppermint, you may also want to try its less common relative spearmint for a sweeter, mellower flavour.

Chamomile

Chamomile is incredibly soothing, especially during times of stress and when the tummy is upset.

Chrysanthemum Blossoms

The chrysanthemum is an important herb in both Japanese and Chinese traditional medicine. Some of the compounds in chrysanthemum are flavonoids like luteolin, apigenin and acacetin, choline and vitamin B1. It is also a good source of vitamins C and A, niacin, folic acid and pantothenic acid and is also rich in calcium, magnesium, potassium, iron and phosphorus. Chrysanthemum tea can help detoxify blood and calm the nerves. The herb also helps to correct imbalances that may affect the liver and also helps in dealing with kidney function, thus supporting their treatment.

Rose Hips

Rose hips are high in vitamin C. They are also said to ward off headaches, which are a common side effect of poisoning and detoxification.

Parsley

To further praise this wonderful herb, like Japanese green tea, parsley is rich in vitamin C and is said to freshen the breath. Parsley is rich in poly-phenolic flavonoid antioxidants, and has been rated as one of the plant sources with quality antioxidant activities. Additionally, the herb is also rich in many antioxidant vitamins, including vitamin A, beta-carotene, vitamin C and vitamin E.

Fresh herb leaves are also rich in many essential vitamins such as B5, B2, B3, B6 and B1. These B-vitamins play a vital role in carbohydrate, fat and protein metabolism by acting as co-enzymes inside the human body.

Lemon Grass

In addition to its culinary usage, lemon grass offers a wide array of medicinal benefits and is in extensive demand due to its antibacterial, anti-fungal and antimicrobial properties across South-East Asia, as well as the African and American continents. The health benefits of lemon grass include relief from stomach disorders, insomnia, respiratory disorders, fever, aches, infections, rheumatism and oedema. The defensive antioxidant activity of the lemon grass herb helps in maintaining cellular health, nervous system, healthy skin and immune system, while also aiding in detoxification. It helps to combat fatigue, anxiety and body odour. It is a source of essential vitamins such as the B-range (see under 'Parsley'). It also provides minerals such as potassium, calcium, magnesium, phosphorous, manganese, copper, zinc and iron. I love lemon grass tea!

Red Clover

Red clover is a wild plant belonging to the legume family. It has been used medicinally to treat many conditions like respiratory problems and skin irritations. It is believed that red clover purifies the blood by acting as a diuretic (helping the body get rid of excess fluid) and expectorant (helping the lungs clear mucous), and very important again by helping to cleanse the liver. Red clover has many natural nutrients including calcium, chromium, magnesium, niacin, potassium, thiamine and vitamin C.

Herbal Blends

There are many brands of detox blends, teas and tisanes out there. Some are recommendable, some aren't; often enough there are artificial flavourings, especially in tea bags. Make sure they come from reputable companies and are organically grown and blended and don't have any suspicious ingredients or added sugar or sweeteners! Tea bags must also be organic, very often they have been treated or bleached, and you will find plastic tea bags as well, which you do not want to use. I much prefer to use loose dried herbs and flowers which I pop into a tea-egg or ceramic tea sieve, over which I pour the hot water and leave it to steam (covered) for up to 10 minutes. Then remove the sieve/tea-egg and enjoy!

Please do not use plastic or foam cups to drink from!

Polystyrene foam cups contain styrene – a chemical compound that is increasingly suspect. In the 12th edition of its Report on Carcinogens, the National Toxicology Program (NTP) stated that styrene is "reasonably anticipated to be a carcinogen", and the International Agency for Research on Cancer has classified styrene as a "possible human carcinogen". And most plastics leach hormone-disrupting chemicals.

Summary of Suggestions

Buy as much organic food as you can, and start using the above listed products; do not go overboard with too many different fruits or vegetables to begin with, and don't think you have to have a fantastic variety of foods! It will take a bit of time if you are not used to eating a lot of vegetables and fruit.

Reminder: avoid sugar, and especially artificial sweeteners and alcohol. Reduce the amount of coffee and tea you drink. I know well how much aviators love to drink lots of coffee! Wean yourself down to 1-2 cups a day and use organic produce. If you do that you have already done a whole lot for your system.

Drink plenty of fresh energised water. I often hear: I can't drink water! I'll say bluntly: Get used to it! You water your plants, don't you? Your body consists of about 65-75 percent water, and this needs to be replenished, and during detox uses more of it. It cannot function otherwise. Remember: without oxygen it's about one minute before brain damage sets in, and severe brain damage after three minutes; without water one can survive about three days, before the system starts shutting down. You can do much longer without food.

Make a green smoothie or juice daily, especially if you do not eat lots of vegetables easily. You can get very high quality greens in powder or frozen form these days, which you can mix into your first glass of water in the morning and which, should you be crew or a regular traveller, you can take with you.

You will discover, and become aware of, how sensitive your system has become as the weeks pass. You will notice that your digestion is reacting and you will take note to what it is reacting to in a negative way, and will in future avoid that particular food. That is another reason why I recommend to not go overboard with variety, so you can more easily determine culprits that cause problems. When you do a colon cleanse you should try and do that in your off days, best would be a one week space. If you do the twenty-one day cleanse, you can take the products with you, they offer a travelling set for the portions en route. The liver-gallbladder cleanse must be done at home, it only takes three days altogether, but you want to be in your own space for that.

If you have been diagnosed with Aerotoxic Syndrome and are severely chemically damaged by contaminated cabin air, and have become a case of MCS, you are a person with serious problems for living. If you are still flying or have taken on another job, you will probably not be able to give it up for financial reasons, although you should!

You may have to move. You may lose friends and family. You will probably have less energy, and realising such prospects is not going to be something you enjoy looking forward to. You will need to spend some money and will most likely not get it reimbursed by your insurances. You may not be able to go to stores and other public buildings; you may even become completely homebound, at least for a while. In short, you will have to give up a great deal, or experience the continued deterioration of your health if you go on living as you have been.

I know this sounds very rough, but the good news is, as you give up these things you will begin to feel better. In time, you may even feel really well and energised again. You may begin feeling almost 'cured', however you will have to be careful not to expose yourself to chemicals for the rest of your life.

I know. I did it. Learning by doing. This is often the case when we begin the journey of recovery to health. Before closing this chapter, here is an example of one of my days:

Morning

After some light yoga stretches, shower.
Cleansing of mouth with a herbal rinse (self-made), and nose with salt water.
Two glasses of fresh water with or without fresh lemon juice.
Take my first micro-nutrients.
Big glass of green juice, smoothie.
(Wait half an hour)
Porridge with ground linseed, cinnamon and honey or banana/egg pancake (no flour) with hemp seed.
Herbal tea or water, later 1 cup of organic coffee.

Midday

I go for a walk with the dogs, and then have:
Steamed vegetables with herbs or a home-made soup and in summer mixed salads, nuts and seeds.
Water and herbal teas.
Micro-nutrients.
Perhaps a kefir or yoghurt with some fruit for dessert.

Late afternoon

Spiced chickpea pancake fried in coconut oil with some beetroot salad and lots of parsley.
Or a couscous or brown rice dish with chopped vegetables and herbs.
Fruit.
Micro-nutrients.

I never eat after 6pm.
Herbal tea or water with lemon juice.

Before bed (never after 10pm): cleanse mouth, do an oil pulling, brush your teeth using a paste made from coconut oil and baking soda, and scrape your tongue clean.

If you need help, please do contact me for a personal consultation; apart from further advice for your individual lifestyle you will receive a personalised guide for your detox programme, which includes meal suggestions and recipes, as well as a plan for micro-nutrients.

I hope I have given you some useful information – it may not be complete in the sense of scientific studies; it is information based on my personal experience through all the ups and downs of trial and error by self-help and self-testing, until I managed to come up with a plan that had a lasting, positive effect, which often times can be more helpful. I then applied this to many patients of mine. If I have neglected to provide a reference, source or link to anything you might be interested in and would like to learn more about after reading this, please contact me, I will be happy to help. Of course you can always do your own research.

It has taken me nearly three years to write this book. It took me through many episodes of ill health and very often I practically had to start at the beginning. It is not easy to write when your brain is foggy and plays tricks on you, when you can't find certain words or on some days you seem to have forgotten all grammar, or simply because your head is so sore you cannot think straight. But, not only eating all the right things and adapting dose and variety of my micro-nutrients, the decision to live in the mountains was a very wise one and I feel much better. Fresh, unpolluted air is one of the major key players.

Epilogue

Wind under my Wings

"My Soul is in the Skye."

(William Shakespeare
A Midsummer Night's Dream)

My heartstrings will forever be attached to flying – so (bitter) sweet are the memories. This is also a reason why I want to help aviators stay healthy; I know how hard it is to have to give it up, even more so due to acquired ill health. Looking up into blue skies where aircraft are without a sound to be heard heading west or east to their destinations leaving behind nothing but a white trail, I try to visualise the crew, probably busy with activities to start or end in-flight service, and I wonder where their layovers might be.

Sometimes I still miss checking my monthly roster and packing my suitcase, which is stored in the attic, the crew label still attached to it. I miss the travelling, the friends, the comradery and all the fantastic opportunities to visit new places in all the countries and see the wonders of our beautiful planet, of which there are so many more I haven't seen. I also sometimes miss the airport flair and the opportunities to fly, at least, as a passenger.

But, events determined otherwise in 1997 and I had to figure out a new life. At the time I didn't know how to do that, nor what to do, and the only available transportation presented to me was a leap of faith, and I took it.

It would have helped a lot if I had received the workplace-related ill-health compensation. I have to earn a living somehow, which is not easy, since my health is not improving and I can't take a job; who would want an employee who is allergic to the environment and sensitised to all sorts of chemicals?

But, everything is possible. Although there are lots of things I cannot do: I have to watch what I eat, can't go to concerts or shop in stores without my mask on and I still have plenty of uncomfortable episodes with symptoms that make me feel very ill, weak and unable to do anything – I am still optimistic when looking ahead.

Spring is in the air, it is April 2015. The sun is throwing warm rays across the mountaintops and I will now step outside with my two loyal dogs, Blossom and Daisy, who will bound out ahead of me. And I will stop to take a few deep breaths of sweet, unpolluted, fresh mountain air.

What can you do?

Here are some hints that injured air crewmembers can use to help get a jump on company defence tactics.

1. Be aware of and assure updated medical files. If the files contain any information from childhood to the present that an adversarial doctor can grab onto, embellish or cite as a pre-existing condition, psychological, or otherwise controversial in any way, they should be re-examined, re-evaluated for the condition, and the file updated.
2. For certain conditions such as blood/toxin evidence, a baseline examination prior to or soon after employment should be established and made part of the medical record. Whether you will need this or not for an aerotoxic claim, the information has a good chance of being useful in this polluted world. Periodic updates will also be helpful and, really, a baseline can be established at any time. Baselines for other health conditions besides toxins and toxicants may also be useful.
3. Know the workers' compensation law in your country or state. Learn the statutes of limitations for every stage of legal opportunity and, when necessary, stay well ahead of the schedule.
4. After filing a worker's compensation claim, you, the employee, must be proactive in managing it. The only

person who really cares about the employee's welfare is the employee him or herself. Airlines have among the highest fixed and variable costs of doing business of any industry and workers' compensation is among the highest expense costs on the balance sheet. Measured against low fares, it is a serious target for cost control.

5. Have an insurance plan that covers all eventualities (loss of licence), be sure to read the small print carefully, before signing up for one.

Furthermore:

1. Become a Member of Aerotoxic Association and benefit from members-only advantages and information;
2. Inform your colleagues, spread the word;
3. Sign the petition;
4. Let us, the Aerotoxic Team, know how you are getting on;
5. Let us know what worked best for you;
6. Do not be afraid;
7. Contact us and stay in touch via the blogs;
8. Ask us for help if in doubt:
   Helpline via www.aerotoxicteam.com;
9. If your life has been touched in any way by Aerotoxic Syndrome, please support the work of the Aerotoxic Association, Aerotoxic Team, GCAQE and ToxicfreeAirlines to ensure safer flying for all;
10. And finally: Be a voice! Have a voice!

Acknowledgments

My Thank Yous

My appreciation and thank yous go to you Michel Mulder M.D. for all your help over the past years; to Dr Holger von Stetten and Professor Müller-Mohnsson (†) who took my condition seriously; my dearest friend Brigitte Proll with whom I began my flying career who is always there for me; thank you to 'Bahi', Professor Abou Donia for your very kind and generous support and invaluable work. Professor Jeremy Ramsden for your expertise for my court case. Lawyer Frank Cannon for your generous and very helpful advice in legal matters. Tim van Beveren, investigative journalist, who never gives up and although he is not affected he battles on to find facts and to help the victims get a voice and continues to inform the public with honest, accurate research and publications: thank you for all your help, professional advice and tips.

Thank you to all those busy bees, researchers, advocates and campaigners in the aerotoxic scene who with bravado, dedication and perseverance and through many hardships, never give up trying to bring the message across to the public and keep prodding the aviation industry and all attached industries in the ribs to make changes. To name but a few: Captain John Hoyte, author of *Aerotoxic Syndrome, Aviation's Darkest Secret* and founder of Aerotoxic Association who gave his generous permission to use his website as a source and quote its contents; 'Melvin', who was a mentor for me while writing this book with gentle criticism and advice – thank you; Aida Infante, former flight attendant, also suffering from the consequences of Aerotoxic Syndrome, who against all odds and hardships keeps on fighting for and helping victims, thank you for exchanging information; Dee Passon, also an aerotoxic victim who has done an immense amount of invaluable work to help prove that Aerotoxic Syndrome exists; to Susan Michaelis PhD, former pilot, also Aerotoxic Syndrome victim, head of GCAQE; in memoriam Captain Richard Westgate (†), first known victim to die from aerotoxic health issues and who left his body to science to help find evidence.

Thank you for being my friend over so many years and for your unconditional understanding to Tara Collingwood, aka Ashtara, who helped with never-ending encouraging support and honest comments; Birgit Leiser, Jörgis Carl, Coni Reber. Endless gratitude to the one man who gifted me with the most exquisite year and lasting memories of the time of my life, and for learning to understand my health issues and continuing to share a very special connection with me. I do not want to omit saying a special thank you to 'Khaghla', for your patience and the years you shared with me, you are a wise 'old' man. Everybody who has touched my life one way or the other is cherished.

Last but not least at all, my two beautiful border collies, Blossom and Daisy, who were born in my bedroom in Ireland by a sweet little mother-dog who stood on the step of my cottage door looking for help on Christmas Day in 2002. They stand by my side every minute and every hour of every day unconditionally; in the nights I am up with severe symptoms, retching my insides out, and during the days when I am lying still because I am too weak, in pain and unable for anything else. They comfort me quietly, lick my tears away and lie close by me, warm me and watch over me until I am able to play with them again.

Websites and Contacts

- Aerotoxic Association: www.aerotoxic.org (English)
- AerotoxicTeam: www.aerotoxicteam.com is international with several languages and offers a direct helpline.
- Tim van Beveren, Investigative Journalist: www.timvanbeveren.de
- Unfiltered Breathed-In: www.ungefiltert-eingeatmet.de/ (German)
- Unfiltered Breathed-In; www.unfilteredbreathedin.com/ (English)
- ToxicFreeAirlines: www.toxicfreeairlines.com
- Toxic Cabin Air: www.Toxiccabinair.com
- International Health Forum IVU – Germany. Dedicated aerotoxic page: www.ivuev.org
- GCAQE: www.gcaqe.org
- Laboratory ProHealth Medical: www.prohealth.nl
- Raymond Singer PhD, neurobehavioral toxicology and forensic expertise: www.neurotox.com
- Brodkowitz Law: www.brodkowitzlaw.com
- Injured on an Airplane?: www.injuredonflight.com
- Pintas and Mullins law firm: www.pintas.com/airline-toxic-fumes.html
- Holiday Watch: www.holidaytravelwatch.com
- Flight Global: www.flightglobal.com
- The Aviation Herald: www.avherald.com

Contact:

Avalon Aerotox Consultancy specialising in

Ill Health issues resulting from exposure to Contaminated Cabin Air on Aircraft, Environmental Ill Health, Toxicology and MCS, Holistic Complementary Health and Stress Management, Education, Personalised AeroCrew Detox programmes, Nutrition.

WeBreatheEasy© Health Camps in combination with:

Workshops: please email* me for information

I am available face to face (on site), email*, skype or phone**

www.aerotoxic.org

www.aerotoxicteam.com

www.aerotoxicsyndrombook.com

aerotoxicangel@gmail.com*

Follow me on Facebook and Twitter

HELPLINE** on www.aerotoxicteam.com

Other book by the author:

Love in the Quantum Space of Time: The Legacy of a Soul Mate

Publisher: Bookhub4you, Ireland, 2011

Article: *Nano Particles and Aerotoxic Syndrome*, 2013

Research Sources and References

1 *Endocrine Disrupters.* Tox Town U.S. National Library of Medicine. http://toxtown.nlm.nih.gov/text_version/chemicals.php?id=65

2 *What's in Your Wine?* Organic Vineyard Alliance Pesticide Fact Sheet. http://organicvineyardalliance.com/pesticide-fact-sheet/

3 *Beyond Pesticides* (Kiwi) www.beyondpesticides.org/organicfood/conscience/navigation.php?foodid=24

4 *Quantifying Exposure to Pesticides on Commercial Aircraft.* 2012, Clifford P. Weisel, Ph.D., Sastry Isukapalli, Ph.D. National Air Transportation Center of Excellence for Research in the Intermodal Transport Environment (RITE) Airliner Cabin Environment Research Program University of Medicine and Dentistry of New Jersey Piscataway, NJ.

5 *List of Countries requiring Disinsection.* United States Department of Transportation. www.dot.gov/office-policy/aviation-policy/aircraft-disinsection-requirements

6 *Acetylcholinesterase Inhibitors: Pharmacology and Toxicology*, 2013, Mirjana B Čolović, Danijela Z Krstić, Tamara D Lazarević-Pašti, Aleksandra M Bondžić, and Vesna M Vasić. www.ncbi.nlm.nih.gov/pmc/articles/PMC3648782

7 Dr Michel Mulder. http://aerotoxic.org/wp-content/uploads/2015/01/AMCIttE.pdf

8 *Health effects caused by Pyrethrine or Pyrethroid Exposure in civilian air crew members*, H. Müller-Mohnssen, Professor Ludwig-Maximilians, University Munich, Germany.

9 *Derived from flowers, but not benign: Pyrethroids raise new concerns.* Weston. http://www.environmentalhealthnews.org/ehs/news/pyrethroids-raise-concerns

10 *Chronic sequelae and irreversible injuries following acute pyrethroid intoxication.* Toxicological letters, 107, 161-175 (further references) Müller-Mohnssen, H. (1999)

11 *Can exposure to organophosphates make people sick?* CDC Centers for Disease Control and Prevention Department of Health and Human Services. http://www.cdc.gov/nceh/clusters/fallon/organophosfaq.htm#make_sick

12 *Research on Multiple Chemical Sensitivity (MCS)*, compiled by Professor Anne C. Steinemann and Amy L. Davis University of Washington from http://mcs-america.org/SteinemanDavis.pdf

13 *Peripheral Neuropathy/Toxic Stress.* Dr Sarah Myhill. www.drmyhill.co.uk/wiki/Peripheral_neuropath

14 *Toxic Neuropathy.* Jonathan S Rutchik MD et al, updated 30.04.2014. http://emedicine.medscape.com/article/1175276-overview

15 *Toxic peripheral neuropathies.* Michael T Pulley MD PhD Med Merits section 3 of 6. Article. www.medmerits.com/index.php/article/toxic_peripheral_neuropathies

16 *Poisons That Make Hair Fall Out.* Mar 21, 2011 by Janet Contursi. www.livestrong.com/article/82586-poisons-make-hair-fall-out/

17 *Psychiatry Is Not Based On Valid Science.* Philip Hickey PhD (Mad In America) www.madinamerica.com/2014/01/psychiatry-based-valid-science/

18 *Low Level Exposures to organophosphorus esters may cause neurotoxicity.* 2002, 27 Dec. Jamal, Hansen, Julu. www.ncbi.nlm.nih.gov/pubmed/12505280

19 World Health Organisation 2010 publishing on disinsectant spraying. www.inchem.org/documents/ehc/ehc/ehc243.pdf

20 *Elimination of Engine Bleed Air Contamination.* Reddall, H., SAE Technical Paper 550185, 1955, doi:10.4271/550185.

21 *TCP (tricresyl phosphate) fact sheet* – New Jersey Department of Health http://nj.gov/health/eoh/rtkweb/documents/fs/3130.pdf

22 *TCoP (triorthoscresyl phosphate) fact sheet CDC* – Occupational Health Guideline. www.cdc.gov/niosh/docs/81-123/pdfs/0642.pdf

23 *Exposure to triaryl phosphates: metabolism and biomarkers of exposure.* 2013, Nov 25, Clement E. Furlong. www.ncbi.nlm.nih.gov/pmc/articles/PMC3839637/

24 *Autoantibodies to nervous system-specific proteins are elevated in sera of flight crew members: biomarkers for nervous system injury.* 2013, Abou-Donia MBI, Abou-Donia MM, ElMasry EM, Monro JA, Mulder MF. www.ncbi.nlm.nih.gov/pubmed/23557235

25 *Health and Flight Safety Implications from Exposure to Contaminated Air in Aircraft.* Dr Susan Michaelis PhD, Sept. 2010.

26 *Aviation Contaminated Air Reference Manual.* Susan Michaelis, Publisher: England: S. Michaelis, 2007.

27 *Cognitive function follows exposure to contaminated air on commercial aircraft: A case series of 27 pilots seen for clinical purposes.* Sarah Mackenzie Ross, Virginia Harrison, Laura Madeley, Kavus Davis, Kelly Abraham-Smith, Tessa Hughes and Oliver Mason. Research Department of Clinical, Educational and Health Psychology, University College London, London, 2011. www.itcoba.net/30MA11A.pdf

28 *Organophosphorus ester-induced chronic neurotoxicity.* 2003, Abou-Donia. www.ncbi.nlm.nih.gov/pubmed/15259428

29 *Elevated Nitric Oxide/Peroxynitrite Theory of Multiple Chemical Sensitivity: Central Role of N-Methyl-D-Aspartate Receptors in the Sensitivity Mechanism.* Martin L. Pall. www.ncbi.nlm.nih.gov/pmc/articles/PMC1241647/pdf/ehp0111-001461.pdf

30 www.mil-pecproducts.com/Documents%5C631_Aeroshell%20Turbine%20560%20MSDS.pdf

31 *The Differences Between an Allergy and a Chemical Sensitivity.* Allie Frownfelter in *Public Life*, 2015. http://unscentify.com/differences/

32 *GCAQE evidence shows contaminated cabin air is real and present threat.* GCAQE Press Release, Dr Susan Michaelis PhD. www.anpac.it/attachments/article/412/120419-CS-GCAQE-contaminated%20cabin%20air%20is%20real%20and%20present%20threat.pdf

33 *Comparison of the Constituents of Two Jet Engine Lubricating Oils and their Volatile*

Pyrolytic Degradation Products. 2000, Van Netten C, Leung V. www.ncbi.nlm.nih.gov/pubmed/10701290

34 *Crew Effects from Toxic Exposures on Aircraft.* 2005, Winder, Michaelis. http://link.springer.com/chapter/10.1007/b107246#page-1

35 *Pathophysiological Effects of Chronic Toxicity with Synthetic Pyrethroid, Organophosphate and Chlorinated Pesticides on Bone Health of Broiler Chicks.* Umesh K. Garg, Asim K. Pal, Gautam J. Jha and Sanjay B. Jadhao. http://tpx.sagepub.com/content/32/3/364.full.pdf

36 *Applied Nanotechnology.* Jeremy Ramsden, Collegium Basilea, 2009.

37 *Nano-Particles and Aerotoxic Syndrome.* 2013, Bearnairdine Beaumont (not peer reviewed).

38 *Air Pollution Linked to Cognitive Decline in Later Years.* July 3, 2014, Dr Mercola. http://articles.mercola.com/sites/articles/archive/2014/07/03/particulate-matterair- pollution.aspx

39 *Mechanisms of allergy and chemical sensitivity.* 1999, Meggs WJ www.ncbi.nlm.nih.gov/pubmed/10416285

40 *Acute Toxicity of Organophosphorus Compounds.* 2013, Christoph M. Morris et al. http://link.springer.com/chapter/10.1007/978-1-4471-5625-3_3

41 *Hormesis: (LOAELS)a revolution in toxicology, risk assessment and medicine.* Edward J. Calabrese www.ncbi.nlm.nih.gov/pmc/articles/PMC1299203/

42 *What Organophosphates and Toxicity disrupt Phase 1 And 2 Liver Detoxification Pathways.* Carina Harkin BHSc. Nat. BHSc. Hom. BHSc. Acu. www.carahealth.com

43 Traditional Chinese Medicine (TCM) – World Foundation www.tcmworld.org

44 Ayurveda – www.ayurveda.com

45 *Acupuncture – Migraines, Tension Headaches Respond to Acupuncture, Acupuncture for tension-type headaches.* Linde K, et al. *Cochrane Database of Systematic Reviews*, 2009, Issue 1.

46 Acupuncture | University of Maryland Medical Center. www.umm.edu

47 Reflexology – www.netdoctor.co.uk/healthy-living/complementary-health/health-benefits-of-reflexology.htm

48 Biofeedback – www.webmd.com/a-to-z-guides/biofeedback-therapy-uses-benefits?page=3

49 Colon Cleansing Internal Cleansing Kit – www.blessedherbs.com

50 Orthomolecular.org – www.orthomolecular.org

51 *Orthomolecular medicine: the therapeutic use of dietary supplements for anti-aging.* Michael Janson. www.ncbi.nlm.nih.gov/pmc/articles/PMC2695174/

52 *Sources of Micro-nutrients (Vitamins, Minerals, Antioxidants)*: University of Maryland Medical Center http://umm.edu/health/medical/altmed

53 *Free Radicals, Antioxidants, Oxidative Stress.* 2005, M. Valko, C.J. Rhodes, J. Moncol, M. Izakovic , M. Mazur www.sciencedirect.com/science/article/pii/S0009279705004333

54 *Treatment with tyrosine, a neurotransmitter precursor, reduces environmental stress in*

humans. Banderet, L. E. et al. *Brain Res Bull.* 1989 Apr; 22(4), S. 759-62.

55 *Free radicals, antioxidants and functional foods: Impact on human health*. 2010, V. Lobo, A. Patil, A. Phatak, and N. Chandra. www.ncbi.nlm.nih.gov/pmc/articles/PMC3249911/

56 *Redox signalling (cross-talk) from and to mitochondria involves mitochondrial pores and reactive oxygen species*. Andreas Daiber 31 October 2009, Revised 15 January 2010 www.sciencedirect.com/science/article/pii/S0005272810000435

57 *Antioxidant effect of Withania somnifera glycowithanolides in chronic footshock stress-induced perturbations of oxidative free radical scavenging enzymes and lipid peroxidation in rat frontal cortex and striatum*. Bhattacharya A, Ghosal S, Bhattacharya SK. *J Ethnopharmacol.* 2001 Jan;74(1):1-6.

58 *Search for natural products related to regeneration of the neuronal network*. Tohda C, Kuboyama T, Komatsu K. *Neurosignals*. 2005;14 (1-2):34-45.

59 *Cholinesterase inhibiting withanolides from Withania somnifera*. Choudhary MI, Yousuf S, Nawaz SA, Ahmed S, Atta UR. *Chem Pharm Bull* (Tokyo). 2004 Nov;52 (11):1358-61.

60 *Effect of theanine, r-glutamylethylamide, on brain monoamines and striatal dopamine release in conscious rats*. 1998 Yokogoshi H et al.

61 *Curcumin Antioxidant and anti-inflammatory properties of curcumin*. 2007, Menon VP, Sudheer ARA www.ncbi.nlm.nih.gov/pubmed/17569207

62 *Curcumin Detoxification and antioxidant effects of curcumin in rats experimentally exposed to mercury*. Rakhi Agarwal, Sudhir K. Goel, and Jai Raj Behari. *Journal of Applied Toxicology*. 03/2010; 30(5):457-68. DOI:10.1002/jat.1517. 3.17 Impact Factor

63 *Wheat grass juice in the treatment of active distal ulcerative colitis: a randomized double-blind placebo-controlled trial*. E. Ben-Arve, et al. *Scandinavian Journal of Gastroenterology*, April 2002: 37(4): 444-9. Pubmed.gov.

64 *Evaluation of the antioxidant activity of wheat grass (Triticum aestivum L.) as a function of growth under different conditions*. S.D. Kulkami, et al. *Phytotherapy Research*, March 2006; 20(3): 218-27. Pubmed.gov.

65 *Buckwheat Honey Increases Serum Antioxidant Capacity in Humans*. 2003, Nele Gheldof, Xiao-Hong Wang, Nicki J. Engeseth Copyright © 2003 American Chemical Society

66 *Glyphosate's Suppression of Cytochrome P450 Enzymes and Amino Acid Biosynthesis by the Gut Microbiome*. Anthony Samsel and Stephanie Seneff , *Pathways to Modern Diseases*, 2013, www.mdpi.com/1099-4300/15/4/1416

67 *Carcinogenicity of tetrachlorvinphos, parathion, malathion, diazinon, and glyphosate*. Kathryn Z Guyton , Dana Loomis, Yann Grosse, Fatiha El Ghissassi, Lamia Benbrahim-Tallaa, Neela Guha, Chiara Scoccianti, Heidi Mattock, Kurt Straif, 2015, on behalf of the International Agency for Research on Cancer Monograph Working Group, IARC, Lyon, France. www.thelancet.com/journals/lanonc/article/PIIS1470-2045%2815%2970134-8/references

PRINTED AND BOUND BY:

Copytech (UK) Limited trading as Printondemand-worldwide,
9 Culley Court, Bakewell Road, Orton Southgate. Peterborough,
PE2 6XD, United Kingdom.